Praise for

Alone Together

❝Monica shares through her own experience of how bravery sets a victim free. This is a great story!"
—**Bob Proctor,** From the movie "The Secret"

❝Wonderfully written! _Alone Together_ takes the reader through a creative journey of releasing negative beliefs while replacing them with empowering thoughts."
—**Peggy McColl,** New York Times Best Selling Author

❝Monica Da Maren's book is full of stories that will make you feel emotions you thought you forgot how to feel. They will all inspire you to face your own past troubles, forgive yourself and find the strength to start healing . . . Monica's writing reads like a warm conversation with a dear friend . . ."
—**Jennifer Colford,** International bestselling author, Managing Mothering

❝Monica shares a story of tragedy overcome by courage, sorrow overcome by joy and fear overcome by hope. Her story is one shared by many people, one of belief in the lies of their past. In this book, Monica reveals her way out of those lies and into a fulfilled, meaningful life! Let this book be an encouragement to you, to be brave and to discover who you really want to be; even if others try to tell you that this person does not exist."
—**Sarah Thatcher,** Teacher

Alone Together

Discovering the secrets to build a winning self-image

MONICA DA MAREN

158.
/
DAM
C 1

Published by
Hasmark Publishing
1-888-402-0027 ext 101

Copyedit by Philip S Marks
DocUmeantPublishing.com

Book layout by DocUmeant Designs
DocUmeantDesigns.com

Cover by Patti Knoles
VirtualGraphicArtsDepartment.com

First Edition, 2015

ISBN: 978-1506131436
ISBN-10: 150613143

Dedication

To MY BOYS that keep my soul full of happiness every single day.
For everything and forever to my hero, my mom.

Contents

Foreword

FROM THE MOMENT I met Monica something special stood out for me. At the time I would have never guessed what her story was about. Like most of us we have two parts to our self image. The one we portray to the outside world and the one we keep hidden inside.

In my work I've met a lot of people who have struggled with the remnants of their abusive past but when I started to work with Monica I noticed something very special. I've never seen anyone move through their healing at such a rapid rate.

She's told me it was my belief in her that got her moving because she didn't believe in herself. I'm so happy that I saw what you will now get to see. What a remarkable woman she is!

Monica has seen both sides of her self image and now she is living an authentic life and big things are just beginning for her. If you are struggling with a past that holds you back, this book is the key to letting go.

If we all could just believe what Monica learned to believe, that what happened to us wasn't about us, it just happened to us, then you can truly be free.

If you want to be free this book will release you. It will make you cry, it will make you mad but in the end, you will realize even you can be free of your past.

The truth will make you free! Monica's story is a story of truth, of pain and now joy!

Doug Dane
International Sales Director, Thinking Into Results
Proctor Gallagher Institute

Preface

I WAS STANDING in my kitchen, leaning against the counter, sobbing hysterically as tears streamed down my face, unable to catch my breath. My stomach was churning, my hands covered my face, and my hair was falling out of my bun. I was crying and I had no idea why. Tears ran from my eyes like water from a dam that had burst and they kept spilling down to the floor. This was a cry that I had been needing to have for many years; a cry that came out of my broken soul. It stemmed from something I knew I had to acknowledge for a long time which I was now ready to deal with.

My husband must have heard my heart-wrenching cries as he came to me and put his arms around my shoulders. Slowing the torrent of tears just a bit I looked up at him as he comforted me and said, "Please honey, just let it out, don't hold it in anymore." for he knew I had needed to do this for quite a while.

I reached for a cloth and buried my face into it. I was very confused, not knowing exactly why I was crying. It went on for hours, sobbing all day. I kept saying, "I don't know why, I don't know why I am crying," shaking my head. Deep down in my soul this explosion of tears had been bubbling just beneath the surface for quite some time. During this crying catastrophe, which I refer to as the end of the pain, I received a phone call from a friend. I had known this friend only a short time but we had connected strongly since the moment we'd met. As I debated whether or not to pick it up, because of the state I was in, my husband encouraged me, "Answer it! He will help you."

I picked up the phone and spoke to my friend, telling him a mysterious piece of my life's puzzle. I took a deep breath and said, "Years ago, a good friend of mine choked me, and he wanted me to pass out. I was scared and didn't know if I was going to wake up ever again."

My new friend reassured me saying, "It is good to let it all out, expressing the pain and the hurt you felt, whether it's directly to the other person, or through just getting it out of your system. Doing so will also help you understand what—specifically—your hurt is about. Do not suppress your feelings, get it all out of your system because the truth will set you free." He gave me some words of encouragement and as always I felt better after talking to him.

I was exhausted from fear and was worn out by the demands and beliefs of other people. I was finally crying for the young girl locked inside of me who thought nobody accepted her fully. I didn't know it at that moment but I was expelling the emotional pain I had been carrying for years. By releasing all of this pain I was finally helping this young girl find her place in the world. I was searching for the one simple answer that would end all my problems and lead me out of this prison of sadness and fear. This one answer would lead me into a joyful life, one that I had only dreamed of living. This is the story about a girl named Stella that overcame the negative beliefs about herself, and how she changed her perception of who she was in order to start living an amazingly fulfilled life as an adult.

-**1**-
Stella As a Young Girl

STELLA WAS AT HOME playing alone with her dolls in the family room. She was five years old, the youngest of three children. She sat and chose outfits for her dolls, lining them up for their beauty treatments. Stella would often study these dolls over-and-over, noticing how beautiful and perfectly they were made. Every curve on these dolls was masterfully formed, and the smallest details on these dolls didn't go unnoticed.

Each of the dolls' eyes was unique and told its own story but there was one special doll that stood out from all the others. This doll's name was Rebecca. The doll's hair was red and thick and fell over her shoulders. Her eyes were brown, and she was Stella's favorite. Rebecca was so special to Stella that the two of them went everywhere together; Rebecca even went for pretend drives with Stella. She would grab her imaginary keys and sit on the bottom of the staircase that led to the bedrooms and place Rebecca next to her, putting on an imaginary seatbelt before starting the imaginary car. She would use her imagination and they would often go to the park or grocery store.

During the drive Stella would tell Rebecca that she could get a treat if she was on her best behavior, because no one wants to see a misbehaving girl. What would people think if she couldn't control her doll? Isn't this what all five-year-olds think about—worrying about what others think? She heard someone coming down the stairs and it pulled her mind back to reality. Suddenly she felt embarrassed, scooped up her doll and moved to one side of the step, leaving room for her big brother, who was three years older, to come down the stairs. She felt embarrassed because she was playing with her dolls.

Siblings fight it's just the natural ebb and flow of family life. Different personalities and ages can play a role, but Stella often saw herself as a rival, competing for an equal share of limited family resources and parental attention.

Rivalry was a normal part of growing up, and it drove her parents crazy, especially Stella's mom. She was tired of the bickering that went on between Stella and her siblings. Whether it was due to their unique personalities that clashed, difficulty sharing, or striving to get attention, it would often be difficult for her mom to decipher who was at fault. Stella's sister was six years older and she thought her big sister was the greatest; she admired and looked up to her.

Stella wasn't always the most rational of human beings, especially being the youngest child. Sometimes, she found the smallest issue and turned it into a major battle, straining sibling relationships to the breaking point.

She knew it was completely normal for siblings to get into arguments from time to time. Whether they're squabbling over who's the fastest runner or bawling because one of them dared to breathe on the another, but when she felt the fighting escalate to the point that she was becoming emotionally or physically tormented, she wanted it to stop. Repeated hitting or "torturing" behaviors (for example, incessant tickling, teasing, or belittling) were all forms of sibling acts that she endured and detested. Sometimes they squabbled because they were simply sick of spending too much time together.

Stella's mom was tired, like many moms were tired, doing so many things at once and barely coming up for air. Stella's father worked many hours to bring in what he could so that she could stay at home with the children. Their dream was to save enough money to return to Italy where they came from. Her parents had been born and raised in Italy. As newlyweds they made the brave decision to board a boat to immigrate to Canada and start their new life. As exciting as this may sound, for them it was terrifying, leaving their family, friends, language, and home. Getting over the homesickness took many years for both of her parents. Homesickness, as her mother described it, is much like grief—the stages and emotions are remarkably similar. Stella's parents mourned the death of their former lives!

There were more job opportunities in Canada and her parents had decided to go there for a few years to accumulate money and then move back to Italy, but this never happened. They ended up getting comfortable and stayed the rest of their lives in Canada, only to visit Italy occasionally. Stella saw her parents work very hard but they never quite attained the work-life balance they had hoped for. They did the very best they could for their children.

When Stella was the one who would start the fights with her siblings—it was usually for entertainment, attention, or just to see if she could win a small victory? Picking on each other became a daily routine. After one such incident with her siblings, Stella went back to see her dolls. She picked up one of her least favorite and ran into the bathroom! She was so angry that she acted on an impulse and cut the doll's hair off. Ha, she thought, now you're not perfect! How does it feel to look ugly and not like the others? She looked at the doll, realizing what she had just taken away from her. The long blonde locks were on the floor and there was no turning back. The doll would have short hair forever. Suddenly she regretted what she had done, she knew the blonde locks could never be brought back again. Something was taken away that should not have been. The hair represented a part of the doll's beauty, part of its personality, a beautiful feature that was part of its creation.

Sitting at dinner that night the whole family ate

and shared how their day went. The chatter amongst everyone was of no interest to Stella; she was captivated by her own thoughts. Being the youngest of three kids, she often felt like her stories were not important. She was sensitive, and felt things more intensely, processed things on a deeper level, and was very intuitive. Although being sensitive also made her care way more, she had a big heart for her family and loved them unconditionally. A sensitive soul sees the world through the lens of love. People told her she was sensitive, that she bothered people, and that she got in the way of things, not to intentionally harm her but to point out what she was doing wrong. When she heard this she would internalize it, as if this is who she was meant to be, not knowing at that age that she could have the ability to control her own thoughts. She believed these people when they told her these things about herself.

When she acted out, it was her cry for attention, as she needed to feel connected to people, whether it was a good connection or a painful one. That's where Stella's difficulties began. She learned at a very early age that being the youngest meant you got picked on. Her sister, being older, was always able to do things that Stella wanted to do but couldn't because she was too young.

Her sister was able to wear makeup, choose her own clothes, hang around with her friends, and certain chores were only for her. If her sister knew this at the time, she would have gladly handed over the chores to her little sister with pleasure. Her sister also loved to sleep in the dark but Stella was terrified by it. She would ask her sister every night to turn on a night light but she always snickered at Stella or said she was a crybaby for being afraid of the dark. Although her intention was not to hurt Stella, most nights she cried herself to sleep. Her sister was able to hear her, as they shared a room together, but chose to pay no attention to her. She started to feel invisible, as though she wasn't important and began to believe at times that she couldn't even be seen.

She had a habit of keeping her glass close to the edge of the dinner table and often knocked it down. This became a pattern. On that night once again she spilled her drink because she hadn't put her glass in front of her plate but rather beside it and had knocked it over with her arm. This annoyed her parents, for it caused more work to clean up the mess and they had told her numerous times not to do it.

"Stella, how many times do we have to tell you? Put your glass in front of your plate and you won't knock it over?" her father fumed.

Stella's heart raced as she thought to herself how foolish she was. She stood up to grab a cloth to soak up the spill. Hearing the disappointed and frustrated sighs coming from her parents, and seeing them shaking their heads made Stella feel silly for having done this yet again.

There were many traditions her parents passed along to Stella and her siblings. She believed these traditions were more important than ever. Italian Sunday lunches were the best example, a unique experience she loved. As her family came together she could feel the importance of it, something Stella thought everyone should try at least once in their life. Certainly Italian food and culture go hand in hand, for Stella's parents Italian food is not merely a means for survival. Food defined them. Her mother took great pride in bringing the best possible food for the ones she loved the most. It belonged to their history and culture.

Her father was a man who worked a lot and very hard. It was rare to have him home at night for dinner. He built homes and worked long hours at his job which was very labor intensive. He would leave early in the morning before any of the children would wake up. Stella's mom would wake with him to have breakfast together and also make his lunch just to spend some time with him. She knew he wouldn't come home again until well after the kids were all asleep in bed.

On the weekends he would be exhausted from work as he was trying to give his family the very best life he could. He often worked on Saturdays as well and if he wasn't away at work he would be working on a household project. There wasn't much quality time with his children, and Stella understood that his mind was always focused on work because his heart was to give them a better life. When she heard him speak of his job she often heard him talk about how hard he had to work, which made Stella sad to see her father so worn out by necessity of working hard for money. She often wondered why he didn't change jobs or careers if he didn't like it, although she didn't realize at the time there were not many options for him that he would have been willing to try.

On special occasions, usually on Sundays, they would go to the beach to relax or go to amusement parks. Bringing the family together to have a good time was sacred time that she cherished. Stella and her siblings respected their father so much but also knew if they had crossed the line, their father got a look in his eye and they knew meant that they had disappointed him. He was an authority figure to the family and he represented strong family values that reinforce the idea that a family sticks together through anything.

The words that her mother said after Stella spilt her glass of juice would affect her for many years. They were words that could never be taken back or forgotten. They were words that would change the way Stella would see and feel about herself. Even though her mother had intended them as a joke, Stella took them as actual fact. Unfortunately, it was a story her mother had heard when she was little and now she passed it on to Stella.

"Where did we find you?" her mother asked, shaking her head. "I'll tell you where we found you. We found you in a garbage can! Someone threw you out on the street. Your father and I went out for a walk one night, and we heard a baby crying in a garbage can. We looked inside and found you. Someone threw you out and we felt sorry for you and brought you home." There was laughter at the end of that statement but

Stella didn't realize it was a joke.

Stella felt very confused. Did she hear that right? She thought this was horrible, she felt crushed in her heart after hearing this news about herself. She felt like she couldn't breathe, like she'd been punched in the stomach. This 'joke' immediately became part of her identity, part of who she believed she was on the inside.

She left the table and ran to her bedroom where she threw herself onto her bed and began crying hysterically.

This new belief she had about herself affected her instantly. As she buried her head into her pillow she had images of herself as a baby in a dirty, disgusting bin, alone. "I am garbage, nobody wanted me. I don't deserve anything good because I am no good," she thought she was a waste of time.

That night her heart was broken, and she felt tormented and confused. At some point that night she eventually fell asleep from the sheer exhaustion of the emotional agony and she had a dream that would follow her for many years. She would dream this same dream throughout her childhood and even well into her adulthood.

The recurring dream that Stella had was one in which she couldn't see herself, yet a girl just like her was flying towards a wide field of grass and towards a tree that stood all on its own. The sun was hiding behind the clouds, and it was warm. As she floated slowly towards this tree she felt herself getting drawn into it. The field of grass seemed like it extended endlessly.

As she flew closer to the tree she could see more of its details. It had a wide base and trunk with thick bark and the branches on the tree were covered completely with leaves. The top of the tree was perfectly round, and the leaves were vibrant green. Around the tree, there were a few dark circular patches that were spread out evenly, making it look imperfect.

Stella wondered what those patches were, and thought that if they were not there this tree would have been the most beautiful thing she had ever seen. This tree had a sense of peacefulness to it. It looked strong, as if it had survived for many years on its own. As Stella got closer, she realized these dark patches on the tree were not leaves, but she couldn't quite make out what they were. Nonetheless, she was frightened because all of a sudden she had a feeling that surged through her body that something dangerous was surrounding her.

Feeling her heart pounding, and wanting to fly backwards she tried but couldn't. Something wouldn't let her, trapped in the dream, she had no other choice but to fly towards the tree that now petrified her. She flew close enough to it to gain a clear view of what was in the tree and all of a sudden she saw the skulls. These skulls were moving as if they were alive. They appeared to be searching for a way out. It was bizarre—terrifying! The skulls had no eyes; the sockets were empty, and each one was looking at her, telling her a story, crying out for help. These images terrified Stella, and being unable to fly away from the tree, she was stuck, almost frozen, hovering over it as the scary skulls stared back at her. Their bony mouths were moving as if the skulls were trying to say something to her.

Unaware that her body was moving around in the bed wildly, Stella woke up in a panic. Her heart was racing and she was unable to catch her breath. Her face was covered in sweat and she looked over to her sister, who was fast asleep. Stella quickly looked around for some sort of comfort and she found Rebecca, the doll that never let her down. Holding Rebecca close to her heart, she prayed that this empty feeling would soon fade away.

In the course of time Stella carried on the best she could after the comment that she had been found in a garbage can. What had been revealed at the dinner table was not talked about again for quite some time. Stella truly came to believe that she had been thrown out into the waste bin as a baby. Often she would think of her real parents and wonder what she had done to be thrown out. She developed the belief that she deserved to be tossed away for some reason, but couldn't understand how someone could put a baby into the garbage. She wondered if she cried too much as a baby, at times her family would say to her that she cried for nothing, maybe that was it. Stella decided that from now on she would hold in her tears as much as possible so this family wouldn't throw her away as well. Many questions and assumptions swirled around in her mind. She wanted to find the courage to ask questions but was too afraid to hear the answers.

Stella kept more-and-more to herself, and little-by-little she fell into a hole of sadness and pain. The sibling fighting and teasing each other on purpose annoyed her, but the one thing that wounded her above all else was her belief that she was garbage, the feeling that she was nothing, and someone hadn't loved her enough to keep her.

Stella continued in the role as the baby of the family and was always told she was the one who got in the way of people, and that she was too young to do anything or may it be this was the only thing she decided to hear? She was trying to get her own way, which meant fewer responsibilities and more opportunities for fun, but being the youngest she often found that she wasn't taken as seriously or given the independence she craved. Youngest children often rebel as a way of distinguishing themselves from older brothers and sisters. Stella wanted to be different from the rest.

Over time she learned to detach from the pain as best as she could. Her family life was generally the same, it was "normal"—whatever that meant. Her father continued to work a lot and her mother was busy keeping the kids occupied while she did the house chores. Sibling disputes continued and she had a very hard time getting close to either her brother or sister, not because they didn't want to, but because she felt out of their league and that she didn't belong. It was her mother whom she felt the closest to, a connection that they could recognize without saying anything at all.

She loved being held by her mother as it made her feel safe. There was a soft side to her mother she admired and idealized her for the courage, outstanding accomplishments, and noble qualities she had. She was her hero. On the outside she projected an image of being a strong beautiful woman who kept the household together and excelled at getting the "to do" list finished. Unfortunately, she didn't see herself this way.

The demands of a new immigrant mother was overwhelming at times with all of the cooking, cleaning, cutting the grass, laundry, ironing, washing the floors, making the beds, buying the groceries, and taking care of three kids. Stella often wondered if her mother would one day realize how much time she lost by doing all these tasks to fill in her day. She was so busy doing everything that she didn't see the three little people right in front of her, needing her playtime rather than her service. Something Stella would realize how difficult this is to juggle, one day after becoming a mom herself. Times were different then. Moms didn't spend their days playing and organizing activities with the kids. Her mother did her very best with the life she was given.

Years later, Stella was in her bedroom looking at books, and she was suddenly flooded with emotion, a stream of tears burst forth from a place deep within. She fell to the floor, her elbows on her bed and her forehead resting on her clenched closed hands, praying to be delivered from the hurt she was feeling. She didn't hear her mother walk into her bedroom and it startled Stella when her mother put her arms around her and asked, "Darling, what are you crying about?" There was a look of love in her eyes and a deep concern, and once again a special connection passed between the two of them. Her mother wiped the tears away and cupped her face with her hands, saying, "Please tell me, sweetheart."

For the first time since she had been told that she had been found in a garbage bin, Stella was ready to talk about it. She swallowed hard and looked at her mother, finding the courage to ask she finally crackled, "I was found in a garbage can. Why do you think they threw me out?" The hot tears immediately burned down her face again.

Her mother's face looked confused at first not knowing what she was talking about, but then she gave a look which told Stella her mother had remembered that comment. Her mother's face turned pale, and took on a look that Stella had never seen before. Her mother's eyes opened wide and she shook her head back and forth. "No," she recalled. "No! You didn't believe that story, did you? Honey, that was just a joke. I remember I was fed up with you that night. It was just a saying that people used sometimes when they got frustrated with their kids. It was something I heard as a child too." And with that she hugged Stella as hard as she could.

Stella was stiff and felt no comfort. She had believed for a very long time that she had been found in a garbage bin, and now she was confused by what her mother said. That was a joke? She thought, and her heart sank.

"Stella, look at me," her mother said with concern. She found it hard to look into her mother's eyes at that moment because she felt all mixed up with emotion. "You belong in this family. We did not find you in a garbage can. We love you so much and want the very best for you."

These words meant nothing to Stella and, none of her mother's words felt comforting. It was hard to see her mom so upset and she believed her mother truthfully regretted saying those words to her but the anguish Stella felt was deeply ingrained in her being and could not so easily be shaken from her identity.

The nightmare of the skulls in the tree had been coming to her regularly now. It frightened her to go to bed. She hated having these nightmares, and had no idea how to make them stop. She would cry herself to sleep almost every night hoping the terrifying images would stop, so she could finally feel safe.

– **2** –

Internal
Self-Talk

AFTER HIGH SCHOOL, Stella went to college to get a degree in business. She was determined to do something big with her life. Her mother had always told her she would do something extraordinary with her life. While her friends stayed in high school an extra year, Stella decided to do something different from her peers. She would leave her friends and go to college on her own. This was a very hard decision for her because she wanted to be around her close friends, and especially her best friend of eight years. The two of them were inseparable and they had many good times together, but then things changed and they grew apart.

Stella's dream was to go to beauty school but her father advised her not to go, even though this was where her passion lay. He was concerned about the job of a hairstylist, as the hours were long, and she would be standing all day. He also emphasized he thought the pay wouldn't be great and he believed the work would drain her.

Her father knew what hard work was all about. Building homes was labor intensive and he had always worked long hours himself. Her father told Stella over-and-over again to get a degree in business, just in case she didn't like being a hairstylist, so she would have something to fall back on. This gave Stella the fuel she needed to prove him wrong, to make him proud. What he didn't know was that she had done her research about the job of hairstyling and talked to people who were in the business. She had gathered as much information as she could and still felt a passion for it. She was on a mission and believed that she would succeed. She went to college as he suggested, primarily to make him happy but also because perhaps one day she might possibly own her own hair salon.

College was not what she expected, and she didn't like it at all. The courses were somewhat challenging and she didn't feel any connection with the students in her classes. The two years spent studying at the school went by at a snail's pace. She hated most of it and regretted making the decision to go only to please others.

That summer after graduation she worked two jobs so she could pay for her the actual education she wanted—beauty school. During that time she worked fourteen hour days between a factory and a drug store. This left her barely any time to see her boyfriend Jacob whom she had gone with since high school.

They were crazy-in-love with one another and they made the most of any chance they could to be together. They would make an effort to get together during lunch and dinner breaks, and he would come see her on weekends; they soon became inseparable. They both knew it would only be this way for the summer while Stella was saving money to pay for her schooling. She stopped worrying, and doubting that Jacob would leave her and she had faith that things were going to work out, this wasn't how she planned it, but it was how it was meant to be. She was planning to attend a private beauty school in September and she had to work these two jobs to pay for her tuition.

Her boyfriend was very special to her. She had never felt this kind of connection with anyone in her life. What Stella felt seemed indescribable. He was someone who knew her, the good, the bad, and the ugly and still accepted her wholeheartedly and unconditionally. For her that meant the most pure kind of love. He never once tried to change her; he made her feel as if she was the most important person in his life and worth his time. She felt this true love had touched her mind, body, and soul. They had met their last year in high school and stayed together for many years right up until they got married.

That summer flew by and September came quickly. Beauty school was very different from any school she had ever attended. It was fun, the people were great, and Stella felt she had finally found a place where she belonged. Things came easily for her, when she was doing what she loved it seemed effortless! Even the science and chemistry behind coloring the hair, which some of her classmates found challenging, came easily to Stella. She went to school each day excited, happy, and looking forward to learning. She knew intuitively that this was what she wanted to do, make people happy about the way they looked and felt.

The next ten months of school flew by and there was a job waiting for her when she graduated. She was determined to finish the three thousand hours that were required for an apprenticeship as fast as she could, and that meant working every shift that she possibly could. She wanted to start getting her artistic hands on peoples' hair, transforming them into more attractive versions of themselves. The thought of being able to change the way people felt made her feel even more joyful and empowered. What a gratifying feeling that would be, she thought.

Stella also often wanted to change her own looks completely and become someone else. She wanted to give up being the person she had become, for she didn't like what she saw. Over the years she had been through a lot, and she felt her body was flawed and damaged. Stella wanted to become a person who could stand up for herself and be strong enough to be who she really wanted to be—a woman living free and happy, not one who felt scared and unworthy.

The next step she wanted to take after her apprenticeship was to build up a clientèle, and this would normally take approximately five years of full-time hours. But Stella had something to prove. She had to prove she wasn't a waste; she could do something with her life. As a result, she worked hard and built up a full clientèle in just a little over two years.

Life was good, she was twenty-two years old, working at a job she loved, and meeting all sorts of people was truly gratifying. Most adults she knew disliked their jobs, and she was lucky enough that she had found what she loved to do at an early age. To make matters even better, she had been dating Jacob for four years, and they were talking about getting married. She wanted to be fortune and special enough to be blessed to become a wife and a mom. She shared with Jacob many of her feelings and emotions about life and found that he never once judged her or thought about leaving her because of what she had gone through. Life couldn't get any better than this, she thought. Stella had wanted to get married and had known from the moment they met that he was the one.

Looking back at a particular event in her life, she recalled a moment when she lay in a hospital bed after she was involved in a serious car accident. The paramedics had rolled her on a stretcher into the hospital where her parents were already there waiting for her. The look in their eyes was of deep worry and panic. Stella had been the passenger and her close girlfriend was the driver when their car was speeding as they rounded a bend in the road. The car went off onto the shoulder, spun out of control, and flipped over multiple times before landing upside down on its roof. They were thrown around violently, Stella felt the seat belt biting into her chest and it knocked the wind out of her. The sound of raining glass echoed in her ears as an airbag exploded in her face.

Dangling in midair with the belt digging into her skin she suddenly felt pain all over her body. She believed it was raining as she could hear a slow dripping but when she opened her eyes she realized that it was blood falling from her. She had totally blacked out and had no idea how much time had passed.

Stella slowly turned her head to face her friend terrified to learn whether she was alive or not. She locked eyes with her friend as they stared blankly at each other, trapped in the confusion and chaos of the moment. All of a sudden, panic started to kick in for Stella and she was in a frenzy to unbuckle her seatbelt. Somehow her arm found the way to the buckle but was slipping from her blood wet fingers, where was the blood coming from? She pressed the button and felt her body drop down. She managed to slowly slither her way out of the crushed window feeling the glass scrap against her body. The car was only a few minutes outside of the city, and it was dark out. She was able to crawl out of the car and in the distance she heard the sounds of the ambulance coming to their rescue.

While recovering in the hospital from the accident and dealing with the pain that coursed through her body, Stella was informed by the doctors that she would forever have back and neck issues. She would be able to live a normal life but would certainly feel the effects of the damage that was done to her that night. She would have to undergo procedures and injections to block out the pain.

Lying in the hospital bed, she ran her hand through her hair and was mortified at what she felt in her hand. A handful of hair came out, and then another, and another. Her hair kept coming out in clumps. Due to the trauma and shock that her body endured during the accident, she lost a lot of her hair. Stella's hair was part of her personality, something that people found interesting about her. She liked to do different things with it especially changing the color, but now it was taken from her. All of a sudden her mind went back to when she stood in the bathroom at the age of five, cutting off the hair of her least favorite doll. Now she knew what that felt like.

During her time of recovery in the hospital, Stella was talking to her mother about her boyfriend Jacob. They had just been dating for a month and she told her mother that she knew she was going to marry him; she knew he was the one. She had the ability to understand and knew this would happen, something inside of her told her it would come true. Her mother brushed it off because they had only been together for a couple months then. Her mother knew that young love can sometimes be a temporary thing and she didn't think Stella was in a state of mind to think properly. Anything could happen, but in her heart Stella knew that she was going to be with him forever. Of course her mother didn't understand this. She had no idea how Stella felt on the inside, and her mother didn't recognize the intense connection Stella and her boyfriend felt towards one another. But one day her mother would see. Stella had visions in the hospital of her future and Jacob was in it. She was married, to him and she was a successful, beautiful, and passionate wife.

M EET SARA ...
Working in a hair salon gave Stella the opportunity to express her artistic creativity through cutting and coloring her client's hair. There were many options, styles, and possibilities she could try in order to make the client feel good about themself. She knew the trick was finding the right fit for each person's face and head, shape and lifestyle. At work she was very happy, which was not surprising, given the focus of her work and her desire to form and maintain good relationships with her clients. She had learned early on that a bond needed to be created between a client and hair stylist, it was a relationship similar to a marriage.

Open communication, commitment and trust are the keys for the client. Sharing and teaching the client about what the end result should be is important to gain their trust. The client has a certain image in their head of what they want the end result to look like and in order to achieve that it must be communicated clearly. Some clients use pictures to show what they are hoping to get in a style and others use verbal descriptions. A skilled stylist has to be able to tell the client if the style they are hoping for is realistic for them.

Stella had learned that clients would return because of the personality of their stylist—if the appointment was an enjoyable experience. Clients tend to relax more if they trust their stylist, and the customer's comfort during the whole process is just as important as the end result.

Stella took her job very seriously, thinking of herself and her work as an important part of the health and beauty industry. She felt responsible not only for cutting and styling her clients' hair, but also for having a comprehensive assortment of products to use for different hair types.

She learned an interesting thing very quickly. If she gained her clients' trust, they would come for repeat visits and a strong relationship would develop, and voilà, Stella became her client's therapist. They would reveal all sorts of information to her. Stella knew that she could quickly recognize when clients were experiencing difficult situations in their lives, they would tell her secrets they wouldn't share with just anyone. Often the unveiling of those secrets changed the person and how they felt about themselves. There was something powerful and gratifying to know that as a stylist Stella had the power to erase a bad day in a moment because she was able to make her clients feel great about themselves, and it was the hair styling and conversations that made them feel that way.

In some of Stella's client relationships these patient-therapist roles were reversed. She recognized that if she was having a bad day and was feeling particularly down, her clients picked up on her mood and lifted her spirits by simply reminding her of what she is good at. They would complement her about the way she looked, about how great a hairstylist she was, or how they always looked forward to their visits. When she was doing what she loved she felt very happy on the inside, and she found that she would be fully immersed in her work creating the end result that needed to be achieved. Every heartfelt compliment she received helped to remove some of her old beliefs about being a waste and worthless, and for brief moments she would feel good about herself. Stella wanted to figure out a way to stay in that moment of feeling good for a long time. She knew that she had a poor self-image and she needed help to grasp the concept of changing how she felt about herself to come to terms with who she really was.

She had one client in particular named Sara who became her close friend. Stella would count down the weeks, or days until Sara's next appointment, as she felt a special bond with this client. Sara was a bubbly, heart-warming soul who always found the positive in any situation. During their many conversations about life experiences, the two of them realized they had a lot in common; they spoke of wrestling with the demands of a work-life balance and had lots of conversations about health and exercise. She was a top personal trainer at a prestigious gym and she had a lot of knowledge about health and exercise. Stella became very interested in hearing what she had to say!

Sara was helping people change their image on the outside as was Stella. People are always trying to change their outward appearance to make themselves feel better on the inside, when the real work is done from the inside out. Sara knew this and told her that this change is the hardest part for most people. She often hid behind the stylist's chair while coloring and cutting hair, standing so her clients wouldn't see her. She spent a lot of her life trying to hide. Sara was a woman who competed in fitness competitions and used her body as a kind of suit of armor, and Stella came to admire her for her inner strength and power.

Sara was a woman in her early forties, but she definitely didn't look it at all. She took care of herself, and this appealed to Stella, who had always wanted to do the same for herself but held back. Stella's old beliefs got in her way, and she told herself, "I am waste. I don't deserve to take care of my health."

In the past Stella after a particular incident she started to yoyo diet and that sent her body into so much confusion. Up and down on the scale many times. She did so because deep down she was punishing herself with her body, and felt undeserving of being fully happy the way she was. She believed her body and low self-esteem were the main reasons why certain things happened to her. She did work out regularly and she knew that the release of endorphins produced a great feeling within her, but afterwards she compromised all the hard work by eating poorly.

Sometimes she didn't eat enough and even starved herself, or the opposite she ate too much, holding herself back from reaching her goals, which then lead to damaging self-talk and more feelings of unworthiness and ultimately hatred towards herself.

Finally, Stella joined the prestigious gym where Sara worked and took her classes on a regular basis, falling in love with the hard workouts, and the high she felt afterwards. This change also helped her develop a more satisfying relationship with her body because she had never been a particularly athletic person, and staying fit had been a challenge.

In elementary school, she despised physical education classes and remembered plenty of times making excuses as to why she couldn't participate in gym class. She didn't want to change in front of the others girls in her class, as she was ashamed of her body and felt self-conscious. This lack of athleticism followed her through adulthood, as her continued physical pursuits were more about gaining knowledge and understanding of how the body worked, what exercises to perform when you want to improve a particular area of your body.

With Sara's encouragement and uplifting words Stella began to feel more confident in herself. Sara was persistent with her messages of encouragement, texting her often to see how she was feeling and making an effort to teach her how she could think differently about herself. They had such an emotional connection and had become so close so fast, like long lost sisters.

After some time, during the workouts, Stella found herself increasing her strength and endurance, and with that came huge emotional feelings beginning to move through her body, almost like she needed to break down and cry. This embarrassed her and she felt she needed to limit those emotions. What needed to come out was bottled up with years of emotional baggage. Stella knew that she needed to release so many of her pent up emotions from somewhere deep down inside but was just too scared to admit it—her workouts helped her open up her feelings about the issues of her past. While the process of beginning to resolve issues that had long weighed her down was ultimately a mind-expanding, life-enhancing experience, the initial flood of feelings was a little unnerving.

"All the more reason for you to look closer at what caused this emotional release," explained Sara, "what it may be saying about your life, you might embrace this experience, using it to attain insights and to work through deep-seated challenges. When an accident or trauma occurs, the energy from that event enters the body. This external, disorganized energy, the energy of injury, can be forced into the body through either physical or emotional trauma. If your body is unable to dissipate this energy, it isolates and compresses it into a small, localized energy baggage, effectively storing it for later processing."

Stella often experienced emotional release during her workouts, and sometimes these were accompanied by vivid memories of her past. The simple words that Sara spoke lifted Stella's spirits as did just being around her energy. Words that came so effortlessly to Sara made a huge difference in her life. She wanted to learn to stay mindful of how she talked to herself because, as Sara elaborated, "If what we say to ourselves is negative, we will start to believe every word. Instead, it's better to have positive thoughts and believe them rather than the negative ones. You are one thought away from changing your life!"

Stella, wide eyed, wanted badly to change this. She wanted to become more aware of the ways she beat herself up and knew she needed to change the self-talk messages she gave to herself but had no idea how to do this. She had known that the story she was told at five years old was not true but still she carried the weight of the damage it did to her without even being aware of it.

One day, after a particularly hard workout Stella took a few more minutes to stretch, and as she did so she started to hear the words that her clients told her the previous few days at work. Images of their faces and smiles appeared and they said, "You're so beautiful!" "You amaze me!" "You're so lucky, you have a great job!" "You look so nice today!" "You have it all put together." Stella began to keep those words with her.

It's amazing how other people's words can affect the way you feel; she wondered if her clients knew how much their words had impacted her life. Clients would often say to her, "You have it all together, a job you enjoy, a great life, and you're so happy all the time." Some would even say, "Don't you ever have a bad day?"

This is where Stella struggled. She felt like she was lying to her clients, friends, and family. On the outside she would portray to everyone that she was happy but on the inside most of the time she didn't feel happy. There was a nagging feeling inside of her because she felt she was misleading others. There was an emptiness inside of her. She longed to feel on the inside how others viewed her from the outside.

K AREN'S STORY . . .
Stella remembered the day that one of her clients named Karen began sharing her story and talking about her past. The conversation happened after they had known each other for six years. She spoke to Stella about being adopted and feeling like a thrown away child. It was heartbreaking for many years that she was so young and to feel like no one valued her enough to keep her. She spoke from a place of anxiety and fear and it was hard for her to find her place in the world.

"I felt abandoned, rejected, and hopeless, and felt like I lost my identity," Karen admitted. "During the very critical years when a child should feel the most protected, loved, and nurtured, I felt great pain."

This story resonated with Stella as she had felt the same feelings as a child, except the story she was told was a lie.

Karen knew that to others her life on the outside looked amazing. She was a very successful real estate broker, married with great kids, had a beautiful home, and always appeared to be happy but on the inside she experienced the profound heartache of a feeling of never belonging.

One day she explained her feelings to Stella. "What I have learned is we all have a silent internal conversation within ourselves. There is a voice in our minds almost all the time and it is totally natural but I was never aware of it. The way we speak to ourselves can change the way we feel and can change our behavior. If our self-talk is mainly negative and fictitious it can intensify any stress we are under. The one thing with our self-talk is that we don't question what we say to ourselves, often we don't check the accuracy, we just listen to the statements day in and day out. Whether the statements are positive or negative if we hear them often enough we tend to believe them, even if they are not true. We end up accepting them as being true when often they are not. Even when they are not true we blow them way out of proportion."

Karen reassured Stella that she was much better today after a lot of soul searching and healing. She had found self-love inside herself and she beamed with happiness. However, at times she still wondered where and why her birth mom gave her away as a baby, she experienced her bad days from time to time and that was okay. Karen used certain strategies to help her stay in a positive, happy state, like listening to music, meditating, exercising, saying affirmations, and focusing on her family when she was feeling down these usually made her feel better.

She told Stella, "We often think our negative thoughts are only thoughts, but that's not true either.

We begin to believe what we think about and hear in our heads, and it affects us in many ways. The negativity can come from many different sources, especially people who have an influence in our lives. It causes our stress levels to rise, and in our self-talk we become hypercritical of ourselves. It can influence our self-esteem, our levels of confidence, and all of our relationships. Our self-talk is impacted by our beliefs about ourselves, by other people, and by the world in general."

Karen continued on by saying, "I had to look at what I was saying to myself, this was my first step towards changing the negative thoughts I had about who I was. I began to write down the things I said to myself to make me aware of what exactly I was saying, then began to look at the accuracy of how I was talking to myself and if I didn't like what I heard, I re-wrote it how I wanted to talk to myself. I am a visual person so seeing it on paper was very impactful for me."

She concluded by saying, "I would tell myself over and over again that I am loved by my family and I have a something special to offer those around me, I will breathe in all the good emotions until eventually I will find love for myself and believe I am worthy of having all the good that I have in my life. Meditating helps me so much with this."

Stella listened and thought to herself that changing her own self-talk would take some work and it wouldn't change overnight. It had taken many years for her to attain her own level of negative self-talk.

However, she recognized this type of talk became a habit that could be changed with time and with practice. She realized that if the self-talk did change, it would result in her hearing what she so desperately desired to hear about herself, something far more accurate and much more inspiring.

Over time, Stella would start to get brief glimpses of life where she saw herself free of heartache, but just as quickly as those moments came, they disappeared. She knew she wasn't alone and there must be others who felt this way. Even though she wasn't adopted, she experienced the same feelings as Karen.

Stella recalled that often times she thought she didn't belong in her family, she felt like the odd one out. When she was younger she would rather be by herself playing than interacting with her siblings. She would either be in her bedroom or drawing or reading, it was there that she felt most comfortable and able to be herself.

There was a similar pattern that Stella noticed about the clients who had done soul-searching and soul-healing. They all seemed to refer to themselves in positive terms and use words that were not hateful or degrading. Actually, she had heard this many times before but she had never known how to achieve it for herself. Their internal self-talk was positive and pure, and they indicated that as they became aware of how they talked to themselves and found it was incorrect, they began to change it.

These soul-searchers had found a way of talking about their past in a positive manner, and this often included statements about how much they had grown to love themselves and who they had become. They understood that the words they chose to use were very important and when they talked to themselves their words must be flawless. In order for them to be happy about who they were and love themselves they must clear out all the emotional toxins that existed within. Thinking purely flawless thoughts can lead one to personal freedom. Stella saw positive changes in her clients who had overcome their demons.

That evening Stella lay in bed thinking long and hard, and trying to look at the difference between what her clients did and what she did. "How hard could it be to think differently about myself?" Stella wondered. "Surely the toxic thinking could be fixed in no time," she chuckled to herself. It dawned on her how horribly she was talking to herself after she wrote down a few statements down that came to her, and she hadn't realized how bad it was. It had become natural for her to do this. For many years she had repeated over-and-over again in her mind certain phrases that brought her self-confidence down.

She tried to look at her life from a different perspective, the fact that she was sensitive shouldn't have mattered, and sensitive or not this is how she felt. Stella felt she should be allowed to feel her own feelings and not have to worry about what others thought. She felt things more intensely, and cried more easily perceiving this as a weakness.

Making a decision just about anything took longer for Stella because she had to take time to weigh every possible outcome. She could never decide on anything even as simple as what to order in a restaurant. She always wanted someone to make up her mind up for her.

That same night she dreamt of the tree again, and even after all these years the skulls still scared her. She wondered what they were trying to say to her and she wondered why she kept having the same recurring nightmare all through her life. She desperately wanted to break free of the skulls in the tree. That night, finally for the first time, she understood that the tree itself represented all the horrible beliefs she held about herself. Stella visualized the idea in this manner: she was born with a seed that had been planted. The seed grew into a trunk and sprouted branches, but some of those branches grew skulls on them. These skulls, she realized, resembled all her negative beliefs. They were the opinions and concepts she put on herself, and she needed to find a way to remove them.

She made a vow to herself that night that she was going to wake up the next day and be aware of how she talked to herself, and to change what she normally said, speaking to herself in a more positive way. Stella was going to envision becoming a beautiful, strongly rooted tree. She saw that everything she said or believed that went on in her head was "evil doing" within herself.

In order to change the beliefs she held about herself, Stella would need to start by speak positively, and by doing this it would give her the perfect energy her body needed to begin the process to fully love herself.

She came to recognize that if she were to use positive, powerful words as she spoke to herself, she would eventually have a clear vision of a new self and erase the negative emotional voices that lived inside of her.

There might still be people in her life who would give her unpleasant or negative words and if she took them to heart and internalized them they would become part of who she thought she was, and she would start to act and live that way. Even if it wasn't the intention of those people to speak unpleasant words, they still hit and hurt her. Stella could take the words in and have them stay with her, or choose to reject their opinions, speaking only positively to herself, fully believing that she could become a much better version of herself.

Here is what Stella came to realize that night and in the days that followed: How we speak to ourselves will feed our tree roots either evil food or pure food. Our roots don't know the difference between pure or evil but will take and eat whatever we give them. We can either judge and blame ourselves or praise and love ourselves. Either way, it's our choice and we alone can control our thoughts.

Stella became aware of what she needed to do to remove the tree full of skulls from her dreams. To make the tree look strong and healthy she needed to detach the skulls that lived within its branches and fully understand why they were put there in the first place. By digging down deep into the roots of her tree Stella realized she would find roots going out in all directions. This is where all her beliefs lived and the more she fed the roots with evil food the more it affected the tree trunk and crept up and out the branches as it climbed up to the top of the tree.

Stella awoke the next morning and felt like she could finally breathe a little easier. She was about to pass a mirror. She stopped and looked at herself and spoke "I am worthy of feeling happy!" She inhaled deeply and was excited to start a new journey.

- 3 -
Stella, Age 13

REFLECTING BACK ON her life experiences, Stella went to a friend's house for a sleepover. She enjoyed her friends and that night there were four of them hanging out together. They were all thirteen years old and were having fun singing and dancing. Stella sat on her friend's bed and watched her girlfriends, thinking how lucky they were and that they were more beautiful than she was. She envied them as they appeared to be free spirited, something inside of her held her back from fully enjoying herself. She felt regret and only hoped that one day she could feel happy. Her friends seemed so cheerful and she looked up to them, wanting to be just like them.

The other girls wanted to go outside and enjoy the nice day, but Stella wasn't up to it. She wanted to stay inside.

"Come on Stella, let's go!" said one of her friends.

"No thanks, I just want to hang out in your bedroom for a bit. You go ahead and I'll come out in a bit." Stella assured them that it was okay. She was more than happy to sit there and listen to music and look through the teen magazines that were all over her friend's bedroom floor.

One of her friends shrugged her shoulders and said, "Alright, suit yourself. Join us when you feel like it." It wasn't unusual for Stella to do this, her friends were used to her pulling away from time to time.

She heard the girls running down the stairs giggling and singing. Looking around the room she picked up a few magazines and fell onto the bed on her stomach, enjoying the music and reading up on the latest teen celebrity gossip.

Her friend's older brother came into the bedroom, "Hey Stella where's my sister?" he asked. She explained to him that she was outside with the other girls. She had known him for a few years now, he was four years older and was rarely there when she was visiting. Her friend had often complained about this annoying brother who always teased her.

"Oh, okay, thanks," he said, leaving her by herself.

Stella listened to the radio and enjoyed some time alone. Sometimes her friends got so loud and crazy that Stella needed to just be alone for a few minutes before joining back in the fun.

Suddenly her friend's brother walked back into the bedroom. "Why are you in here and not outside with the others?" he asked, sitting right beside her. It was very strange and awkward as there were other places in the room for him to sit. She moved over a little and looked at him curiously. She felt uncomfortable and sat up, wondering what he wanted. He would never come and hang out with his sister and her friends. He avoided them out of embarrassment. The girls would giggle and make fun of him. Stella thought maybe he just wanted to talk and chill out with her.

"So?" he said.

Looking at him confused, she responded, "I didn't want to go with them."

He was making some small talk but Stella just felt uncomfortable. Her voice was shaking and she couldn't find words she wanted to use.

"I'm going to outside now," she said as she stood up.

She was about to go when he told her he wanted to talk to her about something. She was curious about what he wanted to say. She looked at him and asked, "Is everything okay?"

"Yeah" he nodded and cleared his throat, "Um, I am going to ask you to do something and if you don't do it I'll tell my parents what you did here with my sister last month when you slept over, and they will tell your parents."

Stella knew immediately what he was talking about. The girls had been curious to taste some alcohol and had brought a bottle upstairs and all of them tasted some. None of them liked it but they all forced it down, laughing and wondering how people could drink this stuff, and they had ended up getting really loud and silly from the effects of the alcohol.

Her friend's brother had come into the room and figured out quickly what was going on, he took the bottle and told them they would be in big trouble if his parents found out. After he left the room, the girls felt a little scared thinking their parents would find out, some of them started feeling nauseous. Stella didn't want her parents finding out about it at all because they would be upset and disappointed and they would probably refuse to let her take part in any more sleepovers for a while.

Doing what she was told to do, she sat down again on the bed. Feelings of fear and anxiety began to rise inside her body. What were his plans? Not knowing exactly what he wanted from her, she kept her guard up. Being alone with him brought up a feeling of fear she'd never known before.

"Don't worry, I'm not going to hurt you. Relax. You look so nervous," he reassured her. Her heart was beating fast and she was sure he could hear it, it felt very awkward. He took a deep breath and cleared his throat again. "I want you to take your pants off," he calmly said.

"No!" she barked back to him. She wondered why he wanted her to do that.

"I'm curious to see what a girl looks like," he said to her as his eyes made his way towards her. "I'm not going to hurt you. I just want to see, that's all. I promise. You don't want me to tell my parents about what you and my sister did, do you?"

Stella was numb. She knew this was wrong and she didn't want to do it. She looked down towards the floor, trying to think this through a bit, knowing she didn't want to get in trouble either. She felt a stabbing pain inside and wanted to vomit, she stood up and slowly lowered her pants and sat back down. She kept her head low, letting her hair hang around her face so she couldn't see him beside her.

"You need to take off your underwear too," he said, his voice a bit shaky as he talked to her now.

She felt as though she couldn't stand, like she was glued to the bed. He put his hand on her back, urging her to stand up. "Oh come on, don't be so scared I'm just going to look," he grumbled.

"Please don't make me do this." Stella begged.

"It is up to you," he shrugged his shoulders, "if you want your parents to find out or not. Your choice."

She stood up, noticing her legs were shaking, as she did what he asked her. She brought her hands to the top of her underwear and lowered them to the floor and sat back down, folding her arms across her tummy and squeezing her legs together, feeling them shaking. He then moved from the bed down to the floor, saying to her, "When I'm done looking at you, I'll show you mine, I'm okay with that. I'm sure you're curious as well, there's nothing to be afraid of."

He placed his hands on her knees and slowly moved them apart to open so he could have a look at her. Stella closed her eyes as if trying to disappear from the room. Everything was quiet and still for a few minutes. Hoping he had enough, she tried to move her legs back together again, but he stopped her.

"Hang on." At this point tears started streaming down her cheeks, and her whole body began shaking from the inside. She felt violated and hated herself for allowing this to happen. When she felt him back away she exhaled, closing her legs. Standing up, she put her

ALONE TOGETHER / 43
ALONE TOGETHER / 43
ALONE TOGETHER / 43

clothes back on. However, he stood right in front of her, and closed in on her, leaving her no choice but to sit down again. His zipper was at her eye level. When he began to undue his pants and lower them, she looked away.

"You should look, that way you know what it looks like," he encouraged her.

Wanting this to be over quickly she looked at him. Disgust and guilt roared through her body. Stella blurted out, "No!"

He then pulled up his zipper and walked out the door, leaving Stella numb and sick to her stomach, feeling alone and confused.

Kids will seek out attention, whether it is positive or negative, and if they want the attention of others, they know what to do to get it. This goes for adults as well. If a child doesn't receive much attention from parents or friends, they may grow up feeling neglected. These feelings will then form the main drive behind their attention seeking behavior. Children who grow up within an abusive family environment or with parents who are always absent often make them feel over-looked and therefore the child may grow up to be an attention-seeking adult.

After her horrible experience with her friend's brother, self-rejection was starting to consume her. Stella didn't talk to anyone about her feelings or that she was entertaining the idea of hurting herself in some way. She believed she deserved to feel pain. Stella wanted to trust others, but the hurt was causing agonizing emotions within her, and because of that she became used to feeling as though she was being stabbed from the inside out.

- 4 -

Forgive Yourself and Take Responsibility for Your Actions

JANE'S STORY . . .
"Stella, nothing goes away until it has taught you what you need to know." These were the words of Jane who had been Stella's client for over eleven years. She had now begun to cut and style hair from her home, this decision was not an ideal career choice, but after she had kids she and her husband decided it was the best decision for their family. She didn't know whether or not she would like it, but over a short amount of time it turned out to be very rewarding and she found that most of her clients opened up to her much more at home. It gave her the flexibility and work/life

balance she desired since becoming a mother, and she was able to take a break for dinner with the kids and her husband.

Her clients told her all sorts of personal intimate things that they never would have said at the salon as other people were around and could possibly hear. At home it was more comfortable for them to be able to open up and reveal much more to her. The relationships Stella developed with her clients blossomed into much more meaningful friendships.

Jane, who had just finished her hair appointment, taught Stella a life lesson that she would never forget. She had just retired and was excited to start a new life. When Jane was in her young twenties she married the love of her life, or so she thought.

At first, he was all she ever dreamed of. He was a kind, loving husband, he made her feel so special, but about a year after their marriage he started changing. He began yelling a lot and she felt like she had to tip toe around him because she didn't want to set him off. Then he started physically hurting her.

Pushing and shoving came first; Jane knew this wasn't right but thought it was just a rough patch in their marriage. Then it turned into hitting, which left her bruised and started to lower her self-esteem. After several years of this it progressed to much more dangerous abuse where he threw her down a flight of stairs and threating to take her life.

Together they had one daughter who was then eleven years old and it broke Jane's heart that her daughter witnessed this violence and fighting. Finally

Jane couldn't take the damage and stress it was causing anymore to herself and her daughter. The physical
abuse was one thing but once she started noticing the
emotional effects it was having on her daughter she
decided to leave him. Their daughter suddenly became
very withdrawn and her grades dropped significantly.
Jane was scared to stand up to him as she didn't know
how he was going to react however once she expressed
to him that she wanted out of the marriage he never
once tried to get her to stay or go back to hurt her.

"He was waiting for me to leave all along. That was
why he kept pushing me away—he didn't want to be
the one to leave for fear of what others would think
of him. He was so unhappy, he was always concerned
about what others would think of him in anything he
did. I often think to myself why didn't I leave a lot
sooner, it would have saved me so much heartache if
I had had the courage to leave. At the time I didn't
know that I could, I thought I was trapped."

Jane also confided to Stella she couldn't control her
daughter's behavior, she explained to her that there
was non-stop fighting between the two of them.
Her daughter had always witnessed communication
like this and it was all she ever known this resulted
in her daughter developing poor patterns of behavior
because she thought it was how people normally interacted. Jane had done her best to hide how she felt
about the situation in front of her daughter but children understand much more than we realize.

The relationship between mother and daughter de-
teriorated severely after Jane left her husband and she

couldn't understand why it had worsened. Although, she tried to have numerous conversations with her daughter, she was always pushed away. Jane took her to therapy and counseling, but nothing was working. Her daughter would lash out at her, screaming and yelling, and no matter what Jane tried her daughter wouldn't let her get close to her.

"This broke my heart," she admitted to Stella. "I longed to hold my daughter tight and hear what other mothers hear from their children, words of love and happiness. I was confused and didn't understand why my daughter was so hard to parent, and why she was so unloving towards me. I know leaving her father was a good thing for the both of us, I didn't want her to be around and see that unhealthy behavior anymore. So this made no sense to me."

A few years went by before Jane's daughter was able to talk about what had been stopping her from getting close to her mother. Her daughter reached a point in her life where she was ready to talk about what was bothering her. The news that she had heard shocked and baffled Jane, the man Jane married, the man who was the father of their only child, had sexually abused their daughter.

He had taken away part of her innocence that would forever affect her. After hearing this horrific news Jane hit rock bottom, she was completely numb. She had no idea that this was happening to her daughter at all, and she felt a tremendous amount of guilt, shame, anger, and regret. It explained her daughter's behavior, but Jane still had no idea how to help mend their relationship, and she wanted to be close to her now, even more than ever.

Her daughter blamed her mother for marrying a monster and not saving both of them from the abuse. As soon as Jane's daughter was old enough to move out on her own, she did. Throughout the years they were in contact with each other only occasionally but Jane's dream to have a close relationship with her daughter never came, she still hopes that perhaps one day it will.

Her daughter blamed her and said many awful things to her just so she could give her the misery, hurt, and pain she thought her mother deserved. And that is the exact thing that happened to Jane. She took it all on, beat herself up in her head daily because of what had happened and blamed herself for everything.

Jane recalled, "This all started to affect my health. I was always sick, tired, and depressed. My life wasn't improving because I felt so low in spirit and what I had caused my daughter to live through. I went to work in a daze and stayed clear of people, I didn't want to talk to anyone. I kept to myself. I didn't feel like I deserved to have a life, the amount of remorse I felt was unbearable. I even stopped coming to see you for a while as I didn't want to take care of myself."

Stella remembered when she was going through this and how detached Jane became. Nothing Stella could say to her would help. She needed time to heal her soul.

Jane lost herself for a few years but eventually came back. Jane changed from being very withdrawn and tired-looking into a person who was more alive and fresh and had direction in her life. Stella watched as Jane crawled her way out of depression and even though it was a slow process, she eventually recovered. Stella noticed that she was slowly becoming happier each time she came in for her appointments.

Over a period of time it seemed there was a quite noticeable difference in Jane and it made Stella curious to what she had been doing that had so dramatically changed her outlook on life. Jane would come in for her appointments smiling and start telling stories about what was happening to her with work and friends, and how she was turning her life around. Stella admired her for having the courage to take control of her life. This was something that Stella never thought was possible as she had so much guilt buried deep inside her.

Jane explained to her how she inched her way out of her weeping soul, "If you always give your attention to the horror you experienced, you'll never get to know the person you can become. My past was a nightmare to me, it was a bad dream and I was constantly living in it. Yes, the thought of what my daughter went through still disgusts me and I'll never forget what happened. I know it has destroyed my relationship with my daughter and I can't change things for her. I decided to move on as best as I could and not let my past haunt me anymore."

She took a deep breath and continued, "At some point in our lives we may intentionally, or accidentally, let others down. When that happens I learned that we have to quit making excuses and accept them as consequences of our choices. Quit the regret and focus on the repair."

"Jane you need to explain this more to me," Stella was wondering how Jane ever managed to do this.

"Sure" she said. "After I found out what happened between my daughter and my ex-husband I was devastated. I blamed myself for letting it happen to us. How could I not see it? I was so unhappy and in such a deep, dark hole that one night I contemplated taking my own life. I told myself I'd be better off not feeling this pain, but there was something in me that told me not to do it. There was a little bit of light inside of me that hadn't burned out yet. It was saying, "don't take your life. Live, there is more for you to do here in this world!"

The day after I was so shocked about what I had considered doing to myself that I called in to work sick for a few days, deciding to spend the time at home to give myself a second chance to think about what I wanted from life. I tried to think of a way that I could move on with my life, and realized I needed to forgive myself. I had to confront my own fears, and I had to come face to face with all that had happened to me, to allow those feelings to come to the surface so I could forgive myself."

"You did all that in a couple of days?" Stella asked surprisingly, wide-eyed, feeling inspired by Jane's story.

"Oh no," she chuckled, "but it was the start. By the end of that day I was emotionally exhausted from thinking and writing out pages after pages of what needed to be brought to the surface. I made myself a promise that by the time I went to bed I would feel a bit better and would say out loud that I forgave myself, even if I didn't believe it. I began with that single decision. I started small so it didn't feel like it was too much to take on. It was a baby step, but it was a big deal for me. The more you speak up for yourself, become aware of what you want, how you want to live your life, or make your own decisions, the easier life feels to live."

Stella thought about that for a long time, wondering how much strength it must have taken Jane to face her past.

"I have finally realized there is no need to blame myself, at the time I did the best I could," Jane exclaimed. "I realized the abuse was my ex-husband's way of dealing with what he was going through. Whatever that might have been, it was part of his patterns that he developed, and it was what he believed was true. He took it out on our daughter and me. It was my time to free myself from being targeted; I chose not to be the victim anymore. I decided to free that part of me, for I knew that if I didn't it would slowly kill me."

Without warning Stella's nightmare of the tree with skulls popped into her mind and all of a sudden she knew that it also represented that she needed to forgive herself for what she put herself through. In order to remove other skulls she needed to forgive herself and somehow find peace with her past. There were certain steps that she needed to follow to forgive, making a conscious decision to live in the present even if the past still hurt. In order for the skulls to be fully removed she truly had to forgive and believe that the events happened to her and not because of her! Jane taught Stella that forgiving isn't just something you do for someone else—it can also be something you do for yourself. It's saying, "I am deciding to move towards a life that makes me happy and I am worthy of that. I'm moving on to peace and happiness."

Jane had envisioned herself growing stronger from the pain she felt; she didn't want to let her past destroy her anymore. Stella thought about forgiving the people who hurt her including herself. She needed to give herself grace and take the time she needed to do this. She thought to herself that even if she had to say it thousands times before she believed it was true she was willing to try to make that commitment to herself.

Jane had also taught her to become aware that when another person makes you suffer, it is because that person is suffering deeply within themselves and that suffering overflows to others. The person who makes you suffer doesn't need punishment; they need help. This is the message the person is trying to send to you. Jane's story was an inspiration to Stella.

Stella thought back to her nightmare of the tree again, knowing now that how you speak to yourself feeds your tree's roots. How when you speak negatively to yourself the tree will be fed evil food. She remembered that your roots don't know the difference between good or bad but will take in whatever you give them, whether you judge and blame yourself or praise and love yourself will depend entirely upon you. And now she had learned she needed to forgive herself and take responsibility so she could control the way she thought and in doing so she could change the way she felt on the inside.

The next day Stella went to the gym to have a workout with Sara, all the while mulling over the insights Jane had given her. Sara immediately sensed something was on Stella's mind.

Sara walked directly up to her and said, "What's the matter, are you okay?" Sara then gave her a strong hug that could only be described as powerful on so many levels. She had learned that there is more power in a good strong hug than in a thousand meaningful words and Sara's hugs were powerful. Sara tightly wrapped her arms around Stella as if sheltering her with her strength, almost as she was prepared to fight for Stella's safety, Sara always wanted to protect her from her problems. Together they made growly noises, which gave new meaning to the term "bear hug" and they laughed over this time-and-time again. The two had become such a great friends that Sara was like another sister to Stella.

"Yes, I think I am okay. I'm just trying to figure out how to forgive myself for my past and forgive the people who hurt me so I can move on and not live with this unsettling feeling anymore." Stella told her about what her client Jane went through and how she was inspired to do the same.

"I am so happy that you made this choice," Sara said. "Before you forgive the other people you need to love and forgive yourself. It's okay that you put your needs and wants as a priority and take care of yourself first for a change. During this time you need to understand that you may be unpredictable, irrational, and frustrated. You will be dealing with a lot of emotions," she explained.

Stella had known Sara for several years now and during the past year had divulged much more about herself to her friend. She had become a trusted confidant. She never once judged her or blinked an eye at anything Stella said, instead she accepted her for who she was. They had found through numerous conversations that their life stories were similar and with so much in common they became as close as family. The two clicked and were comfortable with each other, neither of them had to pretend to be anyone else and it was as if they had known each other their whole lives.

Stella realized that there are some people in her life that she would connect with on a deep emotional level, people who understand one another perfectly. It was such a great feeling for both Sara and Stella to know they had one another.

"You need to learn to take incredible care of yourself," Sara said. "Put yourself first mentally, spiritually, and physically, and take time for yourself to do what makes you happy. You are taking responsibility for your life. Devote time for 'you' daily, allow your thoughts to project a positive image of yourself and then you will start to forgive yourself without even realizing it. You can start by telling yourself what you love about yourself. Keep it simple and don't stress about it. When I first started my healing journey the only thing I could find that I liked was my toes." Sara said, laughing. "It's true, that's how low I felt about myself, all I could manage to find that I liked about myself were my toes!"

Stella thought this was ludicrous, but also thought this technique would be a lot harder than it appeared to be. She knew it would make her feel uncomfortable but she was willing to give it a try.

"So many people allow fear to get in the way of forgiving or dealing with their past, robbing them of their reasoning, stopping their happiness, or crushing their dreams. It's not right that we should be living a life with obstacles which prevent us from moving forward and achieving our full potential," Sara added.

"It sounds so easy when you say it, but I'm sure when I go and try to put it into action it will be hard to do," Stella replied. "It takes a lot of inner strength to do this but it sounds like I should start with baby steps, with one simple thing I like about myself and then keep adding on to that."

"Yes that's exactly it, keep it simple to start, I want you to see what I see about you, what others see in you, people all over are drawn to you, don't you see that?" I shook my head no, "You'll get there! I have no doubt in my mind," Sara grinned.

Instead, Stella felt like she was living a lie, portraying a happy image on the outside while on the inside she still felt unhappy.

They started their workout and the whole time Stella tried to stay focused on finding something she truly loved about herself. She found it rather difficult to think of anything, and this got her upset. Her eyes were one thing that she wanted to love, people commented on them all the time and she knew there was beauty in them, but she couldn't see it. She only saw weakness and pity in them.

Years before, Stella had been taught a therapeutic technique that if you were able to look into your own eyes and feel happiness you could love yourself on a deeper level. For when a person mastered truly looking in their own eyes in a mirror and loving what was reflected back, it could transform them. Stella knew that she could fool people with the anguish hidden in her eyes while letting everyone else see a smile on her face.

The next few months Stella promised herself that she would take responsibility for her actions and forgive herself while coming up with several different things she liked about herself, repeating them until she convince herself that they were true. Some would take longer to believe, while others would come quickly. She came up with a study ritual for herself to start off with, doing daily exercises like journaling, finding things to be grateful for, taking time to reflect, and connecting with her vision of being happy.

Once she started these rituals she very quickly came to realize that emotions are powerful and they become real the second they appear and one internalizes them. She understood where she went wrong for so many years in suppressing her emotions, as she felt she had no right to have those feelings on a conscious level. For years, she would bury her feelings and they would sit and fester instead of diminishing, they were there waiting to get her full attention. Her emotions became so real, they were at the surface and she could sense them all day long, they wanted to be honored and acknowledged, and the more Stella tried to ignore them, the bigger they grew, silently impacting her life. She could no longer ignore their existence and she knew if she kept suppressing her emotions they would come back and demand her attention even more powerfully.

Stella began to be more aware of being fully in tune with her emotions and this scared her. She was aware when they would begin to rise within her. Sometimes her emotions startled her as they would race through her mind so quickly. She had learned at an early age to bury her feelings and ignore the past but now these emotions seemed to rise up out of nowhere and hit her like a huge wave crashing on the shore.

So often she would hold back the tears, not letting them flow, afraid of the flood that would be released if she simply gave in. Sometimes, she would let out more than she expected and the peace that she would experience was surreal. She did not know it was possible to feel so quiet and still inside.

Mourning for her past was something she needed to learn to do. She knew one day she would release all those deeply buried negative emotions, but for now as she looked at herself in the mirror, she began slowly to see a little beauty in her own eyes. Once one feels beauty on the inside it is then reflected in one's eyes.

---––––––––––– • –––––––––––---

– 5 –
Stella, Age 15

STELLA HAD STARTED WORKING at a fast food restaurant at the age of fourteen, and had been employed there for almost a year. She kept herself busy with school and her part-time job. She liked going to work and having a new set of friends that she could laugh with and talk to.

Stella made friends with two boys, Steve (who was 16), and Pete (who was 17). Steve lived just around the corner from her house and often they would walk, or he would drive her, to work. The three of them became very good friends and would pull pranks on one another at work. If one of them went into the huge walk-in freezer to get something that needed to be cooked the other would turn off the light on the outside and lock the door for a few seconds. They thought it was hilarious hearing the person on the inside scream since it was cold and dark. It became a game between the three of them, and they made up all sorts of pranks.

They also would dance and sing in the kitchen, having a good time, but they also started getting into trouble because of the fun they were having. The manager of the restaurant tried to separate the three of them when they worked the same shift by putting one in the kitchen, one at the drive thru window taking orders, and the other working at the front register. However, this didn't stop their friendship from continuing to grow.

On the weekends they usually closed the restaurant together usually well after midnight. Pete would often offer to drive Steve and Stella home or they would all go out to a coffee shop to hang out. Stella enjoyed their company and even though she would be tired from working so late, she was ready to go and have fun with them.

Steve was the fun, loud, and lively one and he liked to entertain people with his outgoing personality. Pete was the quiet and serious and liked to stand back and observe what was going on. Every now and then, however, Pete would get their attention and surprise them with his funny outbursts and jokes. Their friendship continued, and after some time Pete was put in charge of scheduling the shifts for the employees. He always worked it out in their favor by scheduling their hours so the three of them could work together and they became like "the three amigos"!

Steve and Stella spent more time together because they lived so close to one another, and they would almost always hang out at his house. His parents worked a lot and during the summers Steve was home taking care of his little sister. It was so different at Steve's house, for his parents worked all day and it was just his sister and he. Stella realized how lucky she was to have her mother home and not have to be left to babysitters all the time.

His little sister would watch television or go to the neighbor's house to see her friends, while Steve and Stella chatted together on the porch. Their friendship was the type where you could talk for hours about everything. Steve was very comical and animated and Stella found herself laughing a lot when she was around him. She thought he was cute and sweet, and she liked his smile and caught herself at times having thoughts of liking him.

She tried to stop herself from letting her feelings for him become more intense, and the instant she felt or thought of him as more than just a friend she would snap herself out of those thoughts. She would feel ashamed for even entertaining the idea, ashamed because she felt that she didn't deserve to have a boy like Steve as a close friend let alone a boyfriend.

Pete eventually got jealous of the time Steve and Stella spent together. At first he would joke about it, telling them he was the third wheel. But as time went on, Pete became more serious making remarks to let them know he wasn't joking. Stella knew his feelings were being hurt but thought it was silly that he was acting the way he was.

One day that Stella would never forget, the three friends were all at Steve's house and Steve's parents were at work and his sister was at a friend's house for the day. As it was raining out, they were all watching a movie together inside. Steve and Stella were laughing and joking about how Stella ate her pizza. Pete was quieter than usual and Stella noticed he was staring off into space, and she got a feeling something was bothering him.

"Hey," she nudged him, "are you okay?"

"No actually, you two have these inside jokes," he said. "What's the point of me being here?" he said as he got up from the couch and walked into the kitchen.

Was he jealous of their friendship? Stella wondered and instantly felt guilty. How could they be more sensitive to his feelings? Stella looked at Steve and he shrugged his shoulders. The two followed Pete into the kitchen.

"Pete, we didn't mean to hurt you. We will fill you in. It's not anything major. We tell you about all the important stuff and I miss you when you're not with us," Stella stressed to him. Steve nodded his head in agreement.

"Filling me in is not the same as being there. How would either of you two like it if you were being left out?" He was getting angry, something she had never seen in him before.

She walked over to him and took hold of his hand, but he pulled it away. Stella said, "I was just going to say, sorry for hurting you. We will be more understanding of your feelings." She was worried because he was acting so strangely.

"Listen, I know you two probably didn't realize how I have been feeling, but you have to understand how hard this is," Pete said. "You two spend a lot of time with each other outside of work and I feel left out. My home life has been crazy and I need my friends to help me, not make me feel worse."

His parents were in the middle of a nasty divorce and he was being dragged into it. Stella's heart ached for him. She didn't want to lose his friendship, but he was getting upset over nothing. She walked over to him and hugged him. He held her tight and they hugged for a long time. It felt nice to feel him relax in her arms.

Steve was standing behind Stella and said, "We are sorry!"

They separated their hug and Stella noticed Pete wink at Steve. She turned around to look at Steve, confused, and she saw that he was looking at Pete and nodding. She thought that was strange.

"Stella, can I talk to you privately?" Pete asked.

"Yeah, sure, okay," she said. Stella took a step back and looked over at Steve. He smiled and told them to use his bedroom for privacy as he was expecting his buddy to come by and pick up a movie and hang out for a bit. This way they wouldn't be interrupted.

Stella followed Pete into Steve's bedroom, they sat on his bed and he just stared at the floor. She wondered what he had wanted to talk to her about. She moved beside him in hopes of giving him some comfort, since being friends with both him and Steve brought her joy like she had never experienced before. They accepted her and made her feel special. She did not want to lose either of their friendships.

"This is going to be hard to tell you but I've been feeling upset for a while now because you and Steve have been spending so much time together," he said. "This is not easy for me to say, but— but it's because I like you," he confessed. "I've liked you for a while and I never knew how to tell you."

Stella didn't see this coming at all. She felt like she was blushing and a little smile went across her face. "Really?" she asked, giggling a little.

"Yes, really. I didn't know how to tell you and I was getting upset at you for spending so much time alone with Steve. I felt as though I was losing you to him. I know this sounds crazy and I realize it could ruin our friendship but I needed to tell you," he told her.

"That's silly Pete," Stella said. "I like hanging around both of you and would hate to lose what we have, but I don't know what to say about your liking me. I never really thought of you in that way," she told him honestly. He was opening his heart to her and she wasn't sure how she felt about it.

"You don't have to say anything at all," Pete continued, moving closer to her. He put his arm around her shoulder.

It was quiet for a few seconds, but he seemed so nervous that he couldn't sit still. She wasn't sure what to think, but then he said, "Kiss me."

She looked at him in confusion. "What?" she exclaimed, giggling.

"You heard me. Kiss me Stella." He said, still acting uneasy.

She thought about this for a minute. Maybe a little kiss was harmless. She wanted to feel love and acceptance and he had given that to her. She turned her head towards him and brought her lips to his and they kissed, and she liked it. It sent an electric surge through her body. The kiss was soft, they parted and stared at the floor. Pete's body language was strange. He was shaking his leg and rubbing his hands together and clearing his throat. He seemed so restless. Stella turned and smiled at him, and then he said, "I am glad you liked that, I want more."

Steve's friend had arrived. She could hear them talking on the other side of the bedroom door. She couldn't understand what they were saying but found it odd they were talking right outside the bedroom door. Stella suddenly realized that the room they were in was messy as there were clothes everywhere. It was so unorganized there was clutter everywhere. She was having a hard time thinking, her head started spinning.

Pete turned towards her and kissed her again. They kissed for a while but after a bit he became more aggressive. Stella moved her head back but Pete grabbed the back of her head and continued to kiss her, and when he was done he said, "Now Stella, you can make this easy for yourself or hard—it's up to you."

Stella felt confused. She had a feeling she knew what he meant, but she also couldn't believe he would do this to her. There is no way he would hurt her, it would change everything about their friendship.

"Umm, I think we should just stop," Stella insisted. "Steve's friend is here and it's not right to do this now." She didn't want him to feel rejected but knew this wasn't right.

He took hold of her wrist and snapped, "No, Stella! Steve is fine about us using his bedroom. I already talked to him about it before."

This statement sent wild thoughts spinning through her mind like a tornado. She felt her head going in all different directions. She wondered had they planned this all along?

"You wouldn't have kissed me if you didn't want it. You were smiling after we kissed. You liked it, admit it!" he growled.

With that he pushed her on the bed. The weight of his heavy body fell on top of her, making it hard for her to breathe. Stella instantly got scared and called out to Steve, but all she heard was laughter coming from the other side of the door. She thought of her mother who was just down the street in their home and wanted to cry out to her for help. Stella desperately wanted someone to hear her cries.

"Pete, please don't do this!" she begged him.

"You asked for this, Stella. You wouldn't have kissed me if you didn't. Don't fight it, you'll like it," he tried to assure her.

"I have never had sex before; I'm a virgin," she gasped and she was cold and shaking.

"I know that. Close your eyes. Don't look at me!" he demanded.

"Steve! Help, please!" she shouted.

She heard laughter from the other side of the door, "Nail her buddy, give it to her!" someone shouted back. She didn't recognize the voice, but realized it must have been Steve's friend.

Pete put one hand over her mouth and held down her other arm. His breathing was fast. "You kissed me back, you want this. Now stop talking."

And he was right, in a way. She had enjoyed the kiss for a little while but this was not okay. She knew she didn't want this at all.

"I am going to take my hand away from your mouth. Don't talk or look at me. Close your eyes!" he commanded.

He removed his hand and Stella lay there with her eyes closed, tears streaming onto her face, feeling violated and betrayed. A friendship she thought she could trust was now broken forever.

He managed to lift up her top and expose her chest, with his body still pressing against her. She was dreading what was about to happen. There was laughter and cheering coming from the other side of the door. "Come on, we want a turn too!"

Stella felt numb and trapped. Her mind wandered to her mother, and her thoughts escaped to a distant place, far from what was happening for this brief moment. She went into her own thoughts, thinking again of her mother, and her bed at home which she so desperately wanted to crawl into. A flash of the tree she always dreamt of came to her mind and now it looked mostly black, with just a few green branches.

Stella snapped back to reality very quickly when she felt him take the plunge inside of her. She felt as though she was going to rip apart as he had his way with her. One of his hands was around her throat while the other held her chest. He squeezed his hands around her throat and they felt like hot iron as they closed in a vise-like grip.

The crazed look in his eyes terrified Stella as his grip became tighter and tighter and she felt her breath stopping. She tried to fight back instinctively but was frightened. She dug her nails into his skin but his grip was unyielding. She felt her lungs began to burn from lack of air she began to see dark spots across her vision and she became more and more frantic. Why was he doing this? Stella's thoughts became all fuzzy as the tears of frustration and terror streamed from her eyes! She wished to herself that he would press hard enough to make her pass out.

Then, for an instant he stopped, and it was a relief. She wondered if he was done, but he wasn't. She lost track of time and felt as though she was coming in and out of consciousness. She wanted so desperately to escape. In the distance she heard Steve's voice and it occurred to her that this must have all been planned. She had trusted them, but now she realized that nobody accepted her for who she really was. They had violated their friendship with her.

When Pete was done he collapsed on top of her, crushing her again with his body weight. His breathing didn't slow down as he rolled off of her, got up and covered her with the bed sheet, then left the room.

Stella took notice of how sore she was. The muscles in her legs felt strained and as she sat up she saw blood on the sheets.

The door opened and in came another guy; Stella didn't know who he was. She covered herself back up with the sheet again, moving as far away from him as possible.

"Oh you are cute. Nice eyes!" He growled like an animal at her.

He walked towards her and tugged at the sheet, but Stella gripped it tightly. She was terrified, she had never met him before, and she wondered where he came from and if this was some sort of sick joke.

"My turn now!" he hissed.

Stella screamed and shouted, hoping her voice would carry over to someone who could save her.

The smell of alcohol came from his breath and he looked much older. He had scruff on his face and had a stocky built.

All of a sudden the door flung open and Steve came in and pushed this animal who was preparing to attack Stella towards the wall. He lost his balance and fell. Stella took this as a perfect time to run off. As she ran out of the room she could hear them fighting and swearing at each other. She managed to get dressed and run out the front door not looking back once.

The friends whom she thought she could trust were now strangers, and she didn't recognize who they were. In a blink of an eye they took advantage of her, Stella's whole world of people she trusted vanished. As she walked home, passing the houses she was familiar with and the people who lived inside of them, she wondered what was happening inside these homes. Someone could be begging for help and yearning to escape without being heard. Pete, Steve, and his friend had planned the afternoon just to have their way with her.

She walked inside her home, and Stella fell faint onto her bed, wishing the bed would somehow suck her in and enclose her, burying her deep into its folds. She felt confused and thought she was again in a bad dream, a nightmare, and it was something she knew she wouldn't ever be able to forget. Feeling disgusted, ashamed, and guilty, she headed for the shower, desperately wanting to wash away all the hurt so that it would go down the drain and vanish forever. She wondered how she could let this happen to herself, why wasn't she strong enough to resist or brave enough to fight harder. Turning on the water as hot as she could handle it, she tried to wash away the pain as she thought of those former friends who had just betrayed her. She hoped she could ease the memories by watching the water flow down the drain.

That night Stella cried herself to sleep. She cried for what she had lost, cried for not being strong enough, cried to find the strength to tell someone what had just happened.

- **6** -

Take Control of Your Self-Esteem & Self-Confidence

TRACEY'S STORY...
"One of the things that held me back from pursuing my dreams for many years was my lack of self-confidence." Tracey told Stella.

Tracey was a client of Stella's for over nine years. She was a woman in her fifties when Stella came to know her, and she had been battling a rare lymphoma breast cancer for the past six months. She had just found out that she might have only a few short months to live. Tracey was in excellent shape. She had been a runner and was extremely fit but during these past six months she had seen her weight dramatically decrease. Because of the stress of her illness, the treatments she had to endure, all the worrying for her two children and husband she was going to leave behind,

Tracey dropped a lot of weight very quickly.

She had lost her hair and it was growing back now very slowly, it was soft like baby-fine hair. She came to her standing appointment every five weeks in order to get the few strands of hair she had trimmed around the perimeter. "Just make it look tidy" she would smile, laugh and tell Stella. It would take Stella no time to cut but she always booked the regular time of forty-five minutes for an appointment, leaving them time so they could talk.

Stella never knew if she would see Tracey for the next appointment which saying goodbye to her was always challenging and painful. She told Stella it was a way for her to get out of the house and come to Stella's home where none of her family was around. At Stella's home she felt the freedom to let go of a lot of emotions that she held in at home and while in the hospital. In those two places she kept herself together for the sake of everyone else since she didn't want them to see her sad or in agony, she wanted them to remember her leaving as a strong fighter.

Tracey was sitting in the stylist chair while Stella 'tidied up' her hair she listened intently as Tracey reflected on her life. "It's something we all face to some degree, these regrets in life. I don't think most people realize it until they're about to die and leave their loved ones that having life regrets is a curse.

"I think about the anguish in my own life, the things I should have done differently, the dreams I should have gone out and fought for, but my lack of self-confidence stood in my way, until about five years ago when I started my own business.

"That's when I started working on how I felt about myself. I was tired of letting my low self-esteem stand in the way of so many things I wanted to do, and by taking small steps I started to overcome my fears and was finally able to pursue my dreams."

Tracey always dreamt of opening a unique high-end clothing boutique. She had a different style to her and an eye for putting together outfits that always looked stylish and beautiful. She loved bright bold colors and mixing patterns and fabrics, something that she was able to put her own twist to and loved teaching others how to do the same.

She finally opened the boutique three years ago and it had taken off. She was successful, she was living her dream and she was ecstatic to have felt the rush of achieving her goal before her death.

"Do you remember a few years ago when we changed my hair from boring one length to sassy short and we colored it from brown to bright blonde?" Tracey recalled, laughing as she spoke. "Looking back, that was not like me at all, but I needed the change in order to start fresh."

Stella smiled, "Yes, that was liberating for me, too. All these years I wanted to change your style and you finally let me. I knew it was in you to do it, you just needed to be ready for the change. You told me you were letting go of the old you and needed a huge change in your style. We brought out the new you!"

Tracey agreed, "Yes! I loved walking out of your salon knowing I had started my new journey of becoming what I always wanted to become, a successful business owner. When I think back to the year I worked on starting my business I still had so many fears, but I knew I could beat them. In my gut I just knew it was the right thing for me to do, I wanted to prove to myself that even I could take a risk and succeed.

"Unlike my business, the cancer that has taken over my body and made me limp and frail and I know I can't beat it but at least I will have felt success before I die. This disease is something I cannot beat, but my business has grown at such a rapid rate in such a short amount of time I really think it was because my belief was so strong. I had big plans to push my success even further. The business soared high so quickly like the cancer which also grew quickly, but unfortunately the end result of the cancer is death." Tracey sighed.

Stella had known that Tracey held back starting her dream job for so many years because of her insecurities. She had told Stella this story a few times over the years they had known one another, expressing to her with tears in her eyes how much her peers affected her.

When Tracey started high school she had a terrible time fitting in. She was at a new school because her father had changed jobs and this change in schools was very difficult for her to deal with. It was hard to make new friends and fit in. The job change her father was forced to take made them relocate to a new city, and so she had to start at the new school not knowing anyone. This caused her some anxiety just thinking about it.

The first month in the new high school wasn't so bad, but she was reluctant to meet new people and so she kept to herself. She was very shy and felt self-conscious about the way she appeared. To make matters worse, her face decided to have a major acne outbreak at the worst possible time. This problem made her keep her head low in class or when she walked down the hallways in hopes that nobody would look at her. This also made her an easy target as it made her stick out more in the crowd. Girls slowly started making fun of her, and more and more joined in on the teasing, until eventually it led to her being bullied daily.

Tracey was stuffed into lockers as if she were a rag doll and had no feelings, and she wouldn't dare go into the cafeteria to eat lunch because the 'popular' girls would laugh at her loudly and then people would make comments like, "Tracey, your face is a sin. How can you walk around looking like that?"

She was even spit on, and they purposely tripped her when she walked through the halls. She told Stella she eventually started eating in the bathroom in a stall in order to wait and hide out there until the bell rang to indicate that lunch was over.

She was utterly humiliated during her high school years, and those painful feelings left her in despair and terror-stricken for a long time. Tracey missed every important event that she should have experienced in high school, such as dances, parties, and proms, and all the important things a teenager should get to enjoy and go through.

Her self-confidence took a beating by her peers. Each time they laughed at her or poked her, she would fall deeper into depression and develop a darker more harming self-image of herself. For many years this weighed on her, she never felt happy about herself. Her husband would tell her everyday how beautiful she was, but she never saw what he saw.

It wasn't until her mid-forties that Tracey realized she needed to take control of her self-image. At this time, Tracey was working at a bank and was in a meeting with a supervisor who had a temper. He was frequently under a lot of stress and often burst out at Tracey, knowing full well he could get away with it.

This day, for some reason, he took his anger further and put his hands on her and shoved her out of his office, and that was the last straw for her. She had experienced enough abuse already, she had enough of letting people walk all over her. Tracey had put up with his workplace bullying for quite some time, and had let him take out his stress on her because she wanted to fit in and she did not dare make an issue of this.

She knew this bullying at her work was connected to past events in her life, it related especially to her high school days. She held a certain standard for herself and that's what she lived up to, and at that moment she decided that she would no longer let people walk all over her.

After she endured this indignity at the bank, Tracey decided she needed to change things once and for all, to take hold of her life and live her dreams! She quit her job at the bank and took matters into her own hands empowering herself to turn her life around.

"You can become someone worthy of respect, and someone who can pursue what you want despite the negative words of others," Tracey said. She was explaining to Stella what had worked for her to gain more self-confidence. "I believe that I am worthy of respect from others and I finally got to the point where I believed in myself. I had no more pimples, they had all vanished years ago but when I looked into the mirror all I saw was that young pimply kid, and I knew I needed to take control of my self-confidence and my life once and for all."

Stella had admitted to Tracey that she too knew there was more to life for her, she loved her job and was happy with her family, but inside she felt there was more in store for her. She was determined to figure out what it was that she was capable of. Maybe for Stella it was the simple fact that she wanted to feel happy and content with herself, or maybe once she arrived at being happy with herself she would find there was more to her, something really big she would be capable of.

Tracey continued to give Stella her advice in the hope of reaching out to her before she died. "I learned a couple tricks that changed everything in my life," she said. "I would imagine that a negative thought was a big block, and I would diligently be on the lookout for these blocks. When I saw one, I would kung fu chop it, mentally of course," she chuckled, "break it, and knock it down! Then I replaced it with a positive thought. With this tiny little skill I created a way of making great things happen. I was changing my awareness of myself, I was changing my own self-image."

Stella visualized her blocks and they would be labeled with her negative beliefs, some blocks would be labeled "fool", "I can't", and "unworthy". It would feel so good to kick those blocks hard and shatter them.

Tracey resumed, "Another trick is that I would visualize going into a battle with myself—one who was shy, and one who was confident. The most well informed general knows his enemy inside out; they study them. You can't defeat your enemy without knowing them. And when you're trying to overcome a negative self-image and replace it with a positive image, your enemy is yourself."

"Get to know yourself very well, start listening to your thoughts, get to the core and figure out why you do the things you do. I kept a journal about the thoughts I had of myself and analyzed when I was having those thoughts. I remember staring at the page and thinking, Wow! I really think poorly of myself." Stella was nodding to her "I had these limitations in my mind, and I had to ask myself if they were real limitations or just ones I allowed to be placed there."

Tracey described this with such energy that it carried onto Stella, who could feel her excitement.

"Stella I can see you have greater power of success inside of you, don't get me wrong you are successful, but I think something is holding you back. You need to dig down deep within yourself, and you'll come out eventually with even greater self-confidence than you already have. It's an incredible feeling once you have reached that higher awareness."

Stella sighed and nodded. None of her clients had any idea about her past and how she saw herself. Most of the time she felt as though she was living a lie. There was the "Stella" that everyone saw on the outside but the "Stella" that she thought and felt on the inside was very different. Sometimes the true Stella would appear, those were the good days when she would see herself as everyone else saw her. She would feel happy and see the beauty in herself, although tragically it never lasted very long. Sometimes a thought or trigger would pull her right back so fast that it almost felt like she was trapped in this cycle of thoughts forever.

"You have to be positive," Tracey started to tell Stella, bringing her thoughts back to the conversation. "It's more than just thinking positive; you have to put it into action. Action is the key to establishing great self-confidence. It's one thing to learn to think positive, but when you start acting on it and feeling it, you change yourself, one action at a time. You always end up doing what you think about constantly, and so if you change what you do and how you act, you end up changing who you are. I now talk to people in a positive way and put all my energy into action every chance I can. Very quickly I started to notice a difference in myself and I could see that the people I interacted with shifted their attitudes."

Stella smiled at Tracey, she felt better just by talking to her, it gave her hope but Stella was at a loss for words. She struggled to see how she could do the same in her own life. How is that possible? she wondered.

Stella admired Tracey and how she dealt with her cancer. Tracey told her over-and-over that one day at a time is enough. She wanted to live in the present and make each day so beautiful that the loved ones she was leaving behind would remember her kind words and courageous actions. She wanted to enjoy the last bit of time she had left in this world.

It was so odd, when she found out she had cancer, she felt as though she had just started to live her life, and now it would be taken away from her. Tracey had found herself at the crossroads of her life, and she could either, let this disease get her down or she could find a way to live one day at a time.

Stella remembered what Tracey said just after finding out about her illness. "For me, getting through treatment meant blocking any thoughts of the future, because the future meant declining health and increased suffering. Not something you want to think about. I tried to think about what's needed to get me through the day, the next round of chemo, the next blood test, or the next scan. What can I do for myself to make it a better day? What can I do to make myself feel better today? I put the blinders on. This is where I am. This is how I'm going to make the best of it. I wanted to spend time with family and travel. This is how I should have been spending my days before I found out I was sick, living life, not being stuck in old beliefs about myself."

Stella wrote in her journal that night about a new path she would hope to follow. "I will not be concerned about mistakes I've made yesterday, or faults I have, my burdens, aches or pains. Yesterday has passed forever out of my control. I cannot undo a single act I have performed. I cannot eliminate a single word I've said. Nor should I be worried about tomorrow. I will wake up and either the sun will shine or hide behind the clouds. Nothing has happened yet and until it does, I shouldn't fret about it. Daydreaming of a better tomorrow is what I should be doing, not fearing with uncertainty about what might potentially happen. I need to go and make what I want out of life and passionately live my dreams."

- 7 -
Stella, Age 16

S HORTLY AFTER PETE VIOLATED HER, she gained a great deal of weight. This made her feel even more shame and regret. She never told anyone what had happened to her. She thought that if she told anyone what had happened that she would be blamed for it. She remained too afraid to tell anyone because irrational thoughts ran through her head. She thought, maybe she did lead Pete on when she kissed him back and she just keep beating herself up about it. She was afraid of what people might think, afraid of being blamed for what happened and as the weeks and months passed she decided to never tell anyone, as it wasn't worth the pain of living through it again.

Gaining weight made her unhappy, although she used food as a way to deal with the pain, and to ensure that guys would not be attracted to her or look at her favorably. She ate to control her emotions and numb her thoughts and feelings. Anytime she felt remorse or shame she would binge and eat large amounts of food in a very short time in a totally mindless state.

She knew it was wrong and unhealthy, but she couldn't stop herself. She ended up in a lot of emotional pain from eating and the binging also caused her to feel agonizing pain.

Usually within minutes of the binging, the feelings of regret and embarrassment would boil up within her. It was a vicious cycle. She rewarded herself with food; comforted herself with food; entertained herself with food; and became obsessed with food. However, she didn't know she was obsessed, and much like her odd beliefs, the madness became normal.

She would also sneak big mouthfuls of food from the pots of her mother's cooking when her mother briefly left the kitchen, she would hide food wrappers and eat when nobody was watching. It became a game to her. She wanted to see how much she could eat in the shortest amount of time. When she snuck food from the kitchen she would very quietly lift the lids to the pots, taking in spoonfuls at a time and not really chewing the food, but just taking a few bites, enough to break down the food so she could swallow it.

Stella would try to eat any chance she could get, often going into hiding to do so, cheating herself out of happiness. She numbed herself of any feelings she had and brought more pain to herself due to her feelings of worthlessness. This was all about control, and self-loathing. It was a way to hurt herself and make herself feel disgusting and unworthy of having people look at her.

Food became Stella's drug of choice. She got just as wasted from overly processed sugary, fatty, and salty food as others got from doing illegal drugs or alcohol. There were times when she even passed out in a food coma.

There were plenty of days she would not eat at all at school as she didn't want to be seen eating in front of other people. She would get embarrassed if others saw her eating, she was told watching a fat girl eat was not an attractive sight. People were starting to make fun of her. She would go hide in the library and eat her food or sit silently inside a bathroom stall, afraid to be found, and afraid to face humiliation if someone saw her eating.

Stella's addiction reached a new level while she worked at the fast food restaurant. Thankfully, the boy who violated her left the restaurant where they worked shortly afterwards. When she showed up for work, everything changed, including the friendships she made. She became withdrawn, and the more weight she put on the more withdrawn she became.

She worked as a cashier and also in the kitchen but it got to the point where she would sneak a burger and tell the floor manager that she was going to the back freezer to get some supplies that were needed. She would open the big heavy steel door and as it closed behind her it would click shut, but she never once turned the lights on inside. Instead, she hid and ate in the dark. There she found herself in the dark freezing room, unwrapping the paper that held her addiction, using something other people needed to survive, as a tool to destroy her body.

Just a short while ago she would be laughing in this freezer when they played jokes and now she was in tears standing there harming her body. At her age, Stella could never have known that this would result in years of misusing food to feed something other than hunger burning deep inside of her. Secretly eating her hamburger, barely chewing and crying at the same time, brought Stella to a dark place of self-destructive feelings. She took pleasure knowing she was doing something wrong to her body as she hated herself to her very core.

After she finished eating the stolen food she would go back onto the floor and work, silently plotting the next chance she would get to sneak away and eat. When she was working in the kitchen it was easy to find a way to eat food and she would do this every chance she got. At the front cash register she couldn't sneak in food as easily but she eventually found ways to go about it, and she became utterly consumed with finding ways to eat while working.

Stella fell deeper and deeper into a circle of feelings of remorse, shame, and regret. When she worked at the drive-thru window it was easy to get food to eat. She would sneak something into a paper bag and put it to the side, when she got a chance Stella would then take the food out of the bag munch on it and then tuck it away into a corner where she would grab bites as often as she had the chance to do so.

The kitchen staff sometimes messed up orders and they would toss orders that were made wrong into a separate bin to be thrown out. She would often ask to take the bin out and then return to it hours later to open the wrapped food and gobble it down. Or, to be more accurate, to gobble the trash!

She didn't see herself as an addict; she knew what she did was wrong but she didn't think it was an addiction. To her, being hooked on drugs or alcohol was an addiction. A recovering drug addict or alcoholic could avoid the places or people that triggered their addictions. But Stella had to eat daily. She couldn't avoid food, it was everywhere. Food became her friend and was always near her no matter where she went.

Over time she sank lower and lower into an empty pit of unworthiness. She ate as a way to escape from her feelings and her life. Along with all the eating came all the guilt over what and how much she had eaten. She would beat herself up over her eating habits, but then go and get something to gorge on in order to make herself feel better.

She did more than overeat, she often ate until she became physically sick, and then she'd eat more. She knew in her head that she didn't want another bite, but a hollow feeling within her kept shouting out, "Fill me. Fill me up!" She noticed too quickly her jeans no longer fit, her tops were too tight and that eventually lead to her ordering new sizes for her work uniform and clothes for school.

One day, after a particularly huge binge at her house, she was home by herself and she had full reins to eat whatever she wanted. She ingested so much food to the point where she felt so full she had to vomit. Those memories created within her feelings of worthlessness and desperation. Every binging session was an escape from her thoughts. The minutes she would take to indulge were her break away from the thoughts of her past when she would shift to thoughts of pleasure regarding food. She had full control over the situation but she chose to lose control by eating until she felt as though she wanted to vomit. Her eating became a bigger problem than she ever wanted to admit to herself.

About a year after the binging started, she noticed some small reddish marks on her body. She thought maybe it was a bump or that she had scratched herself, but as she examined it closely she felt a rush of nerves course through her body and an understanding clicked within her. These were stretch marks. She thought to herself, "I have to stop, I am destroying my body." She was in shock and upset at herself.

Stella thought this negative self-talk would be enough to motivate her to stop binging, but there was more to this story. Fear rose all around her, and she felt instant resentment and anger; right at that moment that itchy, burning feeling she was having was her skin stretching and forming stretch marks that would remind her of this addiction to food forever. It reminded her of the sadness she felt, of why she overate, of the rape she'd endured, and all that had been done to her body over the years. She didn't stop binging, in fact, her addiction became worse and her body was quietly being tattooed with tiny pink lines that would never go away.

Permanent marks of the toughest periods of her life will remain a constant reminder of the insecure and desperate girl that scarred her own body. She would be reminded of the pain of that year every time she looked into the mirror. And the most difficult thing to accept for Stella was that one day she would have to learn to love her body. She would have to conquer the issues her weight gain had caused, being violated, and come to terms with the marks on her body.

Stella dreaded taking the school bus because she was getting bigger and she could feel her body touching the seats as she walked past them, and she would stress about where to sit and whether there was enough room in the seat. She didn't want to go to the back of the bus because of one boy in particular who was sitting in his usual spot. He was the bus bully and would torment anyone he wanted, he was cruel to just about anyone. One day it became Stella's turn and from that day on Stella was subjected to his vicious and demeaning comments.

As she continued to look for a seat, with each step she took she heard him call out, "Boom! Boom! Boom! Here comes the elephant!"

In that moment she so ashamed, she felt like she wanted to die and, actually, a part of her did die in that moment. A fake smile swept across her face indicating that she agreed with him and she thought his remarks were funny, but the feelings she felt on the inside were horrific. His words made her feel twice as big as she actually was. The image of herself that she created inside her head was of a girl who didn't deserve any good. She was disgusted with herself and she hated and despised herself. This bullying on the bus went on for weeks, causing her intense emotional harm and misery, shame and embarrassment.

Later she endured another incident from this bully on the bus. She arrived at the school with her lips quivering and she ran straight into the bathroom, hiding in the stall she cried for the years of pain and anguish that could not be held in anymore.

She had thought of purging for a few weeks to lose the weight, she heard of people losing weight this way but she had no idea how to bring herself to start. This, she thought, could become the answer to her problem. Stella never wanted to be humiliated ever again. She couldn't go on with herself this way anymore and made a decision in that moment that she would lose the weight, and quickly for that matter. She placed her school bag on the floor and using one finger opened her mouth and slowly pushed it down her throat. Her body was shaking and blood instantly rushed to her head. After a few minutes of trying someone came into the bathroom and Stella froze. Her eyes were teary, red, and puffy, and she thought she would try it later. She felt as if she had dropped to another level of desperation, and it was shocking for her but it was worth a try if it meant the bullying would stop. But that night when she got home she was able to make herself vomit and she continued to do that in the weeks that followed, in fact, she couldn't stop.

She taught herself that there were techniques to purging that made it easier for her. When she felt the impulse to eat because she felt agitated or insecure, she would eat loads of food until everything seemed blurry and immediately afterwards she would then clear it away by purging. This left her in a state of chaos with a combination of feelings: relief, satisfaction, self-contempt, shame, and guilt. It didn't stop her from purging though. At times she purged only every few weeks, while at other times purging was an everyday occurrence as it depended on how she was feeling about herself. She started to lose the weight and was happy about that, but with that happiness came feelings of loneliness wrapped up in self-condemnation. She desperately cried within herself, "Someone stop me, someone save me! Someone take me away!"

Stella kept dreaming of the dark tree and she fiercely wanted to figure out a way to put an end to that nightmare once and for all. Still, as a teenager the tree nightmare scared her and made her panic, even after so many years. Confused by it more than ever now, she couldn't understand why the dream kept reoccurring. What did she need to do in order for it to disappear from her life?

- **8** -

Grant Yourself Permission to Make Mistakes

NANCY'S STORY . . .
  "I have to keep reminding myself that I don't need anyone's approval. I need to acknowledge I made a horrible mistake and move on." Stella's client Nancy said, as she sat in the salon chair trying to hold in her tears. She came for her appointment and looked tired, withdrawn, and emotionally exhausted. It was about a month since Nancy's husband discovered she had cheated on him. Stella could feel her pain and knew that Nancy wanted her to listen.

Nancy sighed and began, "I am two weeks away from starting a new job. It is a job I was waiting a long time to get, as you already know and my twenty-five year wedding anniversary is also in two weeks. I happened to be out shopping for a gift and I ran into an old boyfriend from when I was twenty-two years old. He had hurt me when he broke up with me, as I thought we were very close and would be together for a long time. He didn't see it that way of course and had ended the relationship as he was going to Europe for the summer and thought it would be best if we were both free. At that time it truly broke my heart." Stella was mixing up Nancy's color and thinking of how Nancy's voice sounded so full of heartache and sorrow.

"Of all the people to run into while I was shopping for my husband's anniversary gift, it of course had to be him! For a brief moment we talked and it was as if time stood still and we were back again when we were dating. We talked, catching up a little and before we left we exchanged phone numbers. Initially, we started to text each other, which led to phone conversations, reuniting old feelings for both of us. In my mind I was gaining the attention that I had wanted from my husband. Attention that I felt he was neglecting to give me. It felt so good and I wanted more of this attention." Nancy paused for a moment to catch the tears that were now falling from her eyes, she let out a deep sigh and continued.

"Eventually, the talking became intimate, really intimate, and the affair began shortly thereafter. During those two months I celebrated my birthday and on the day of my birthday, I was with my old boyfriend."

She had now begun to cry and Stella stopped what she was doing and gave her a hug, brought a glass of water for her, along with some tissues.

At times Stella wondered how she herself deals with all that her clients tell her, some of their problems they told her could be very hard to hear and were emotionally exhausting but she always gave it her best to give them what they needed from her. Her clients are her number one priority. When they are in her chair she gives them her undivided attention, it naturally came out of her to put them first and she believed that is what brought them back to her time and time again; the comfort and how important they felt while they were in her chair.

Nancy continued, "I was happy with my marriage but I think I was bored. I had no intentions of leaving my husband and two children but I genuinely loved the attention that was being showered on me by this man, it was exciting."

She sighed, "Greg just found out about this last week and I openly admitted everything to him. Stella, he is so hurt and upset at me, and he has every right to be. He moved out yesterday and it's been hell since he found out. We decided to tell the kids that Dad will be busy at work for a while and helping Grandma with some stuff at her house, and he will be sleeping there. I feel so lost every hour that passes. I can't believe I have done this." she cried more, now beginning to sob. Stella empathized with her friend and understood so much of her pain.

"I realize that so many memories now are meaningless to my husband, I can say now that he is gone that his love for me was deeper and stronger than I ever knew. I know that now." She wept, "I am not sure how we will end up, but I can only hope that he comes home and gives me a second chance to be together with him."

Stella felt deeply for Nancy and wanted to help her relieve some of her pain. She knew she that it would be difficult for a while, waiting for her husband to decide if he wanted to stay with her or not would be torturous. The rest of the hair appointment continued with a lot of discussion about Nancy's one deep regret. She wasn't sure how she was going to end up. This was her nightmare she was facing, and the burden she was feeling was a heavy one to handle.

Months passed and Nancy missed all her appointments. Stella would call Nancy to remind her of the upcoming appointment and Nancy would tell her she would have to reschedule, or she had to work, or if she missed one she'd say that she forgot about it and sometimes not answer. She obviously needed to take this time to straighten her life out.

During this time, Stella went on about her life—working, continuing to see her clients, and the joy of taking care of the kids and helping Jacob with his new business. In Nancy's house there was misery, shame, and anguish. It seemed amazing to Stella how one person's house can be filled with love and the next person's house filled with darkness and confusion.

People can hide so much under the roofs of their homes, people driving by on the outside have no idea what's happening inside. Much like ourselves how we portray an image on the outside and often on the inside it is completely different. The people in her life had no idea what she thought of herself. It came across that she was confident—she could hide it so well, she felt as though she was living two lives.

Stella found joy in helping everyone else she put their feelings and needs before hers. She feared hurting others feelings and this worried her, she didn't want to let anyone down. She knew that every time she said "yes" to something and didn't mean it, she would end up being unhappy with that decision, since she didn't say what she really wanted to say. Instead, she would try to please the other person. Stella was always in search of personal validation from others to prove she was accepted. She dreamed of developing the ability to speak her mind in a kind but firm manner, to be able to "say what you mean and mean what you say." She needed to learn to give herself the benefit of the doubt, not taking what others did or said personally.

She assumed when someone was directing some form of offensive behavior towards her that she deserved it, she internalized it and was unable to see that it was only a reflection of what was happening in their own lives. It was her impulse to react emotionally, now as she began to learn she never considered that things were about her. She wished she knew how to control her emotions and not jump to conclusions and second guess herself all the time.

This was the funny thing about Stella as she was great at giving advice to her clients and uplifting them, they made that clear to her she had a gift of making them feel better after being in her presence. They viewed her as having a warm hearted soul and Stella wanted to feel that towards herself.

The way that Nancy was able to own up for her mistake and share with Stella was an attribute Stella deeply admired. Many of her clients found that when they came to their appointments it was very easy for them to release their stress by unloading it onto Stella— it was empowering and liberating for them. This made Stella question why she had a difficult time talking about her own sexual abuse to anyone. Each of her clients did things to cope in their own ways, and each person did what they needed to do in order to survive the events of their past. Every person responds to the anguish that they are experiencing in a different way, and there is no "right" way to heal. But Stella learned that the single act of making the decision to heal was a powerful and positive choice. It was making a commitment, a promise to begin a journey that would be the most honorable thing one can do for oneself.

Stella's phone was ringing and she noticed it was Nancy calling after months not hearing from her.

"I am sorry it's been so long." Nancy said, "I've been tucked away trying to save my marriage and deal with the biggest mistake I ever made in my life. My hair is in need of your magic touch." Nancy sounded desperate for an appointment and she remembered the state she was in the last time they saw each other. She wondered if her husband decided to stay with her or leave. "I am so glad to hear from you, you have been on my mind. Yes, of course I can fit you in for an appointment." She said.

The following day Nancy was sitting in Stella's chair, telling her what had happened to her since she and Stella last saw each other.

"Greg came back to me. He took a few months to make that decision and after he told me, I was very happy! I knew it would take some time for the both of us to heal. I was also worn out by all the thoughts I had about myself and how I had negatively impacted so many lives. I needed to find a way to forgive myself and move on. I tortured myself over my mistakes and during the last few months I had to give myself time to learn from it," Nancy said. "Let's face it, whichever route I take in life, I will still make mistakes, I am not perfect. I saw that one approach eats away at you, while the other helps you become a better person."

Stella nodded her head, agreeing with what Nancy said. There were certain things in her own life that she had done and she regretted all the internal damage she did to herself.

"What I did impacted so many people, in all different ways. There may be some people who felt the impact only a little, but there were others who felt it a lot like my family and friends. Greg lost his trust in me, that's huge thing to get over. I took something away from him that was sacred. I hate myself for doing what I did and now I need to live with the consequences and move on. I had to refocus my attention, and yes, people judged me and still do, but I don't need their approval. I need to accept myself. It's not easy, but in order to start living again I have to deal with it or else it will haunt me forever," Nancy told Stella.

While Stella was cutting Nancy's hair she felt an inner part of her start to speak to her. Stella's realization was something like this: Nancy made a dishonorable decision when she decided to cheat on her husband and now she had to acknowledge her mistake. She recognized she also needed to do something similar but she had no idea how this was possible. She wanted to learn that she didn't need anyone's approval for what she had done in her life and why she did the things she did. Life, Stella was learning, was a series of challenges, and she was going to make mistakes, but that didn't mean she had to suffer from those mistakes or struggles forever. Stella recognized that she had the power inside of her to mold her day and her future. No matter how chaotic her past had been, her future was a clean, fresh blank state, and what she decides to do with it is up to her.

"Most of the hard lessons we learn in life we didn't go after on purpose," Nancy said. "In fact, I think the best lessons we learn are usually at the worst times and from the worst mistakes," Nancy told Stella. "This was the biggest mistake I ever made and from this I have learned so much about myself, and what's more,

I will fail at other things in the future but now I know these mistakes took me off course from the path I'm supposed to be on, but only temporarily. It is okay to be off course from time to time. The faster I acknowledge this, the faster I can get on with my life. I can't let it drag me down any more. I need to focus on rebuilding my marriage and be happy with where I am in life and keep moving forward."

Stella began to tell her that she was capable of doing this and it was something everyone should learn to do.

"Stella it is amazing to be able to do this! After talking to my friends I realized I was not the only one who had made a big mistake and was full of regret. I know this sounds funny, and yes, everyone makes mistakes, but talking to others made me understand that the daily thoughts and internal self-talk I was having of 'Why can't I just do anything right?' or 'I am always making mistakes' would bring me down the rest of the day.

"Every person is special and unique in his or her own way and making mistakes are part of who we are. Whether it is something big or small, mistakes are bound to happen. I needed to grant myself permission to do that and then learn to move on. Doing things that you are hesitant about is a great way to start finding out who you really are and the reality is that mistakes are essential to living a healthy life. Without having certain things go wrong or not having everything come out as planned, you won't be able to learn from them and dodge them the next time they occur.

It gives you a chance to point out to yourself that you will do better next time."

Nancy went on explaining that being able to try again or make a situation better is one of the positive components of making a mistake. We have all over-reacted to someone or something, and sometimes the other person then avoided us. Recognizing that you can change the same situation the next time it happens, is a sign that you have learned something, even if you have to apologize to yourself. The next time you get into an argument with someone, or do something you are not proud of, reflect on yourself about what you learned from it and think about what caused your mistake. Use those mistakes as fuel to feed your ambition. Decide in your mind that you will do better the next time!

"Making mistakes is my fuel to be all I can be next time, and if not, then, unfortunately I will make another mistake and learn another lesson. Remind yourself that even if you make a thousand mistakes, you have a thousand and one chances to make it better."

Stella listened closely to her but was still puzzled by how to do this until Nancy explained further, "All the stuff that has happened to me was, well, because I caused it. It wasn't the other person's fault as much as I would like to have been able to pass on my mistakes I had to own up to it and be responsible to change it. Everything that has come into my life is the result of what I have been thinking. I was thinking for a while that I was bored in my marriage and needed some excitement and sure enough it found me. I focused on this and it appeared in my life. Focusing on something so strongly, whatever it may be, good or bad, you can make it appear in your life and that means you can change certain images you have of yourself. You can even think of a new person you would like to become and create it." She smiled big at Stella.

Stella sighed.

- 9 -
Stella, Age 35

STELLA WAS into her eighth month of pregnancy with the third child she would bring into the world. Her first two pregnancies went well and resulted in very easy and quick births, which she impressed herself, but this pregnancy was very different for her. She had medical problems with her varicose veins from standing on her feet all day and her legs looked as though they were bruised from top to bottom, they resembled a roadmap. When she worked she never booked a lunch break, but would grab something to eat whenever she had a few minutes, she liked this pace of work, never finding it boring or tedious.

She was grateful to have gotten pregnant since she and Jacob had such a difficult time conceiving children. They'd endured several miscarriages during the five years they were trying before their first son was born. Before he was born she remembers feelings of sadness when she heard people say life had gotten so boring after kids, all she wanted was to become a mother. She remembered how unfair life was because her siblings had children and she didn't.

She enjoyed being an aunt very much although she felt as though she was being cheated of the joyful experience of pregnancy and birth and also the festivities that came around that. The miscarriages had an emotionally draining toll on her from prolonged infertility, the physically invasive conception process was always painful, and the associated psychological issues and the uncertainty of a successful pregnancy even with help from doctors, stretched her coping skills. She found it difficult to understand why it was so hard to miss someone she had never met, or dealing with her feelings over others peoples pregnancies, especially when they are due around the time she would have been and then later with their new babies. Dealing with other peoples' inappropriate comments, some with the best of intentions, and also dealing with others who have children without experiencing any problems was more than just painful, it was heart wrenching.

It was six weeks before her due date and that morning Stella had a hunch that something was going to happen to her. There was heaviness in her heart that made her believe that something odd was going on with the baby, and she felt very unsettled all morning. She went about her daily routine but that feeling never left her, that inkling that something was going to happen. She wanted to trust her instinct but chose to ignore what it was trying to tell her, it was that voice within; Stella didn't listen to it very often she usually just settled for what was most comfortable. Her instinct had been telling her for weeks that she should slow down and rest for the baby, but she didn't listen.

At that exact moment she had an agonizingly painful contraction that made her think it was time to deliver the baby. It struck her forcefully, making her sweat instantly, taking her breath away, and leaving her unable to call out for help. She was hunched over in agony. Breathing through it as best as she could for what felt like many minutes, she was finally able to catch her breath and call out to her husband. But then there wasn't another contraction.

Stella's contraction was excruciating, it was strange and confused her because it was more painful than what a false labor feels like, which Stella was familiar with and had experienced them before during her other pregnancies. Stella and her husband waited a little while and decided that whatever happened must have been a tease prior to the real birth, which they knew would be coming soon.

Nonetheless, not doing anything didn't sit well with Stella, and her intuition was calling out to her, telling her to go to the hospital and get things checked out.

She felt restless and suspicious and couldn't calm her nerves. Her husband must have sensed this and suggested they go, not taking a chance; better to be safe than sorry. After dropping off their two sons at Stella's parents' house, they went directly to the hospital.

"I feel so silly," she said to her husband, now second guessing in agreeing to go to the hospital. "I bet we are going to the hospital for no reason at all. I'm not due for another six weeks."

"Too bad, honey," He said, "let's go and see what they have to say. And besides, it will give us a chance to talk and catch up," he quipped. He had been laid off from work and had always had a desire to start his own business. Since he was unemployed it forced him to make a decision quickly. He wanted to provide for his family and make them proud. Starting a new business with two children and also a baby on the way was one of the scariest but most exciting choices he ever made. Jacob started a home renovation company, something he had always had a passion for. He had helped friends and family over the years to renovate their homes and he loved looking at the finished result. It never felt like "work" to him.

They arrived at the hospital and went directly to the birthing unit. It didn't appear to be busy, it was very quiet. The nurse's desk was empty and they stood there for a few minutes before someone came to greet them.

"What can I do for you?" the nurse asked smiling brightly. She was middle-aged and looked fresh, as if she had just started her shift.

Stella felt silly and was gearing up to tell her that there was really no reason she should be there but she was there because she had an inkling she should get checked out. "Well this morning I had a huge contraction, it lasted for a few minutes and it was pretty painful." Stella said, looking down and shaking her head in embarrassment and continued, "look, I know

this is going to sound crazy I haven't had another contraction since but this is my third full-term baby, and
my first two labors were extremely quick. I saw my
obstetrician yesterday and he checked me to see if I
was dilated at all because of the pressure I told him I'd
been feeling. He said that he could feel that the baby's
head was very low, my cervix was very thin and I was
three centimeters dilated. He told me this could be
normal since it's my third full-term baby."

She noticed the nurse look at her confusingly. "Ok
dear, what is it that you are here for then?"

Stella continued, "I was wondering if I could be
hooked up to the monitor to see if there is anything
going on, if the baby is alright. I know this sounds
ridiculous but you need to trust me, I have this feeling
that the baby is coming."

The nurse nodded her head, she must have sensed
Stella's concern and worry, she said, "Well, we normally don't assess someone just because they have a 'feeling' their baby is coming. But it's not very busy right
now and as you said this is your third time around
this, sometimes things happen early on. I can put you
on the monitor and have a listen to the baby. Have a
seat on one of those couches for a few minutes."

Her husband had been holding Stella's hand and
led her to the couches. He could see how uneasy she
was, she was fidgeting while she was waiting to be
called. He told her there was nothing to be worried
about but she wasn't convinced.

The nurse called her and handed Stella a gown to
change into and got her settled on a bed. It was eerie

because it was so quiet; it was just after lunch hour maybe the other nurses were still on break. The only bit of noise was beeping from some of the machines close to Stella's bed. The nurse told Stella that the night before there had been complete chaos, every room was full of patients and there was lots of noise and commotion therefore she was thankful today was a quiet day. "Ok, let's hook you up to the monitor." She said.

Stella could feel the baby moving very little but other than that she felt no discomfort at all. "How silly!" she thought. "This is such a waste of time!"

"Your hands are so cold" the nurse said. "Do you want a warm blanket?"

"Oh, yes please," Stella said, without hesitating. That was one of the best things about coming to the hospital. Those warm blankets were soothing and they made you feel more relaxed.

The nurse stretched the monitor buckles around her belly and made sure the contacts to the machine were all hooked up properly.

"Ok, I'll keep you on this for at least thirty minutes, and then I'll come back to see you."

So they sat and waited, chatting talking about the new business and how life was going to change with three children soon. The monitor beeped every time there was a slight change in the baby's movement or heart rate and the chart recorded if there were any contractions and measured how intense they were.

They realized that almost an hour had gone by and yet the nurse had not come back to see her. Stella needed to use the washroom and she asked her husband to find the nurse.

"Nothing has happened on this monitor, I'm sure they will send me home. See, I told you, this was silly," Stella chuckled.

Her husband got up and went to look for a nurse. Stella rested her head on the pillow, closed her eyes and shook her head, thinking this was a waste of time.

A few minutes later he came back with the nurse. "Hi dear," she said as she took hold of the chart paper that was snaked on the floor. "Ok. Let's have a look at this print out monitoring your baby." She tore off the long sheet of paper, inspected it, nodded her head and said, "Ok. There were only a few very, very mild contractions that you probably didn't even feel very much. This is very normal at your stage of pregnancy." She looked at Stella with care, "Dear, I am going to have to send you home."

Stella nodded her head. She thought back to the morning and couldn't figure out what that was that made her think something would happen. "I am just going to use the bathroom before I change back into my clothes," she told the nurse.

The nurse must have suspected that Stella still was still feeling uneasy, so she said, "Listen dear, if anything changes, do not hesitate to come right back so we can check you out again. I will be here until late tonight."

Stella sighed and said, "Thank you."

Stella made her way to the washroom, which was directly across from the bed. She stood up in the bathroom and a contraction hit her just like the morning, the labor became so intense she began to feel panic rising in her. The painful force ripped through her whole body and took her breath away, gasping to breathe. Grabbing hold of her stomach, she tried to call out to the nurse but the pain was so severe she couldn't scream. The waves of contractions continued to wash over her and fear set in. The door handle was close enough, she grabbed a hold of it and opened the door she looked up and saw her Jacob waiting for her so they could go home.

Stella was barely able to move. Jacob rushed to her side and grabbed hold of her arm. He shouted out towards the nurses' desk, "Help please!"

Within seconds the nurse appeared. "What's happened?" she asked, taking hold of Stella's other arm.

"The baby is coming," Stella blurted out, still breathing heavily.

The nurse was urging her to make her way towards the bed that was only a few feet away, but for Stella it was excruciatingly difficult to walk. Every movement she made felt as though the baby would fall out. "I need to check you, dear. We must get you to the bed." Thoughts in her head were loud and clanging. She knew she was in transition, she knew every physiological step of what was happening inside her. She knew these symptoms of the last stage before pushing: the panic, the hopelessness, the intense nausea, the hot and cold flashes began.

They somehow managed to get Stella to lie down and the nurse inspected her. "I need to call a doctor.

You're eight centimeters dilated; the baby is definitely coming at a rapid rate."

With that, she was gone. What was happening? She was just about to be sent home and now she was just about to deliver a baby. Stella still had a feeling that something wasn't right. She heard the nurse making an emergency call for a doctor over the intercom.

Stella called out to her husband in panic, "I'm in so much pain. I need to push!"

He didn't know what to do. He told her he loved her and said the nurse would be there soon, holding her hand tightly.

As the doctor came rushing in he said. "Wow, I hear someone is wanting to make his or her way into this world fast." He said this with a smile as he put on rubber gloves trying his best to keep the situation calm. The nurse was at his side waiting to hear instructions about what to do next.

The doctor checked Stella for what seemed to be longer than usual. He then looked at the nurse and nodded. "Call for help!" he ordered the nurse and turned to Stella and explained to her, "Your baby is breeched and you're at nine centimeters now. We need to get you to the operating room for a Caesarean right now. Whatever you do, don't push!"

Stella felt instantly fearful and confused. Her first two labors with her others sons were so quick and easy. There was no medication at all, now this was a surprise.

"Get a wheelchair for her and rush her down immediately! There's no time to waste. She will be fully dilated anytime now," The doctor said as he ran off to get ready himself for the surgery.

Another nurse appeared and together they all scrambled to put Stella into a wheelchair. At this point she could feel her pelvic opening up and the pain got much more intense. "Please, can't I just push?" she begged, hoping someone could help her out and relieve this pain.

The nurse was now practically running pushing Stella in the wheelchair down the hallway towards the operating room, "No, you cannot! I know it is very difficult. It's too dangerous for the mom and the baby to deliver breech."

She observed the charade through the fog of intense labor. Her contractions were nonstop, her body preparing her to push. Her husband was behind them and she could hear him asking the other nurse about other options.

Were there other options? She felt like she had no choice. They just told her this is what needed to be done and rushed her off. "I am sure that big contraction you had this morning was your baby turning itself. You said it was head down when you saw your ob-gyn yesterday but when this doctor examined your baby's feet were there" The nurse tried her best to give them some clarity.

They made a quick turn to the right and went directly to a very cold, brightly lit operating room. There were other nurses waiting for their arrival, preparing for the surgery along with two male doctors. The nurse explained to her that there would be a need for a second doctor present because of the "situation" was all she said.

Still in disbelief about what was happening and still experiencing the worst amount of pain she'd ever felt in her life, Stella wanted more than anything not to feel so fearful. Utter despair rushed through her as the medical team manipulated her body onto the table, working as quickly as possible. She sat with her legs hanging off the side of the operating table as a man came to her and introduced himself as the anesthesiologist. "I am here to do your spinal and we need to get this needle into you so we can get your baby out. Now, what I need you to do is sit as still as possible when I insert the needle into you." there was urgency in his voice.

The nurse must have sensed what Stella was thinking because she said to her, "I know you're having contractions, but I'll be here holding your hand and you can squeeze as much as you like. It's very important that you sit still."

Stella knew this but couldn't keep from shifting her body back and forth to try to get relief from the pain and agony she felt. Her body was working very hard to naturally let this baby come out, but her body couldn't decipher that this baby couldn't be born naturally. All that her body knew was that it was time to deliver the baby and the doctors decided it was best to stop this natural process and take the baby out through a cesarean.

Stella felt the anesthesiologist rub something cold where the needle would go into her back. She was

shaking so much that she became convinced the anesthesiologist would miss his target with the spinal
block and she'd come out of surgery a paraplegic, she
was afraid of needles especially this kind that was sev-
en inches long. She had absolutely no idea her body
was capable of shimmying that fast. She felt the pinch
of the needle that had gone in and she suddenly felt a
cold rush, that part was done.

They laid her down and other staff were busy in-
serting a cannula into a vein, a catheter in her bladder, a cuff around her arm to continuously monitor
her blood pressure, an oximeter clip onto her finger
to measure her blood oxygen levels, an electrocardio-
graph onto patches stuck onto her skin to monitor
her heart while under the anesthetic, and placing an
oxygen mask over her face.

She held the nurse's hands and the nurse told her
that soon she would go get her husband and bring
him in. Stella thought how worried he must be, not
being able to help her out being on the other side
of the door praying and hoping. She could hear the
chatter of the doctors off in the distance, "If this goes
well, we are going out for drinks tonight," one of the
doctor said. Something was off, something wasn't
right. Stella knew it and asked, "Is my baby going to
be okay?"

The doctor and nurses were putting up the sterile
blue drape above her chest so she couldn't see what
was about to happen to her. One of the doctors came
over while the other started to open her up, he tried
to explain the situation to her as quickly as possible.

"This will be a bit tricky; you are at ten centimeters and fully open. The baby wants to come out feet first, but it's too dangerous to deliver him this way. Now when you're at this point the uterus will still contract as we are trying to get your baby out. You are our priority. We have five minutes or less to get the baby out once we cut you or the baby could suffer some damage." He rubbed her shoulder smiled gently trying to comfort her. "Let's meet your baby."

The procedure was under way, she felt very cold and shaky. The anesthesiologist stood over the top of her and told Stella he was going to give her something more to relax her, and then he smiled. He put a mask over her face that blew out something that made her feel instantly a little more relaxed. Her husband now had entered the operating room. He appeared next to her and kissed her forehead softly. "Sweetheart I'm here now." he said and ran his cold sweaty hand over her face, "I love you."

A male nurse came over to Stella and told her to stretch her arms out to the side and place them on the arm rests, he held one side down and called another nurse, who was male, to hold the other side so she couldn't move them. This way her arms wouldn't interfere with what the doctors were doing. She laid there and saw the male anesthesiologist looking down at her, watching her. She also knew the two doctors performing surgery were male as well. "So many men?" she thought, there was one female nurse off in the distance that she could see recording something on paper. She hadn't noticed there were tears coming out of her eyes until her husband started wiping them away. She looked back at him and thoughts of their life together throughout the past years flashed before her. She loved the magic they held together. Destiny decides who you meet in your life but it's your heart and how it makes you feel that decides who gets to stay in your life.

She felt so much pressure coming from her stomach, the doctors worked as best as they could to pry the baby out. Her body was moving from side to side as they tugged and pulled, it felt as though they were trying to remove a bowling ball.

She wanted to vomit and felt like she was losing her breath. All of a sudden, without warning feelings similar to when she was raped came back to her. Vivid flashes of that horrible day came into her mind. These similar feelings that came back were definitely caused by all these men in this room standing over her, holding her down. She was tied down and they were in control of her body. She couldn't run, she was stuck, and as she lay there helpless she lost hope.

Off in the distance she heard them saying that five minutes was approaching and she knew this was it. She was in horror and felt as though she wanted to die. Ironically she was in labor, bringing life into this world and at the same time she gave re-birth of all these emotions that were locked up for so long, being ignored. She felt something make a switch in her head and her heart. Stella was ready to leave this world and her family behind, ready to give up on her life. She knew her Jacob would be fine. There would be plenty of people to help him out and the kids. She shook her head back and forth looking up at the anesthesiologist, he recognized her cry for help and took her mask away from her face and she managed to say quietly "stop" and he said, "I will give you more stuff to relax you." He placed the mask back on her face tried to knock her out with the anesthetic, but she could still hear people talking in the distance.

She may have passed out but she faintly heard off in the distance the doctor say, "It's a boy, take him to ICU immediately."

After that everything became dead silent. The rush, the frenzy, the buzz and the commotion came to a stop. She wasn't sure how much time went by, maybe she faded in and out of consciousness from the medication. She looked around and noticed her husband was gone but had no idea when he left her side. She could hear the voices of doctors talking while they worked on her, putting her body back together.

"It's all over now," a nurse said, trying to console Stella. "You had a boy. He's in the intensive care unit and your husband is with him."

Stella didn't feel any emotion. Her heart felt heavy, she wanted to succumb and leave this world.

One of the doctors came over and explained to her they were able to take the baby out just in time before severe complications occurred. But in order to get him out they had to temporality lift out her bladder and intestines to make room for them to find the baby's leg that was hiding. One leg was down but the other was stuck behind her bladder, her uterus kept closing in on the doctors' hands as they tried to remove the baby. Stella had no idea what she would have to deal with during the months ahead. She would need an incredible amount of courage.

The next three days at the hospital were a blur to Stella. She was in intense pain and therefore was receiving strong medication because of the severity of lifting her bladder and intestines out to take the baby out. She found it difficult to think straight and her new baby was sleeping away from her in the ICU where they could monitor his breathing. However, Stella found she couldn't bond with her son. All she thought about when she looked at him was that his birth was a big nightmare. She wanted to wake up and be back at home where she felt safe and could be herself.

The weeks that followed were just as hard. She had no desire to do anything, and fell into a depression. Stella should have been happy with a new baby at home, and her other two boys and husband gave her a lot of love each day, but she didn't feel she deserved any of it. On the outside she smiled when family and friends were around, but on the inside she knew that something had happened during the cesarean the familiar feelings she had that day reminded her of events from her past and opened up a ton of emotions that she was going to have to deal with.

The next few months Stella did her best to ignore her pain and emotions that were brought up from her past during her surgery. Her mother was around to help out a lot and it was clear to her that her daughter was going through a hard time. She often told Stella to bury the emotions she was feeling. "Bury the past, swallow it up and move on," she advised her, also telling Stella to focus on her beautiful family and to try to forget what was bothering her.

The nightmare of the tree resumed nightly now, waking in a rush of fear after each dream and hard to fall back asleep afterwards. The tree had changed dramatically it was now completely covered in dark patches, moaning in distress and slowly dying a little every night. The dreams were the worst they had ever been, and Stella knew that in order for her tree to become beautiful she would need to find a way to remove the demons that lived in it now that the truths were coming out of it and needed to be dealt with once and for all.

– 10 –
Quit Worrying About What Others Are Thinking

CATHY'S STORY . . .
Cathy, Stella's client, told her, "I dealt with so much of my past around eleven years ago when I couldn't take the pain anymore. Now you need advice and I can give it to you. No problem!" Cathy was special to Stella. She had known Cathy from the start of her career eighteen years ago. She was good-hearted, had a great sense of humor, and she had a bright, shining personality. Cathy had been through much disheartening child abuse but since dealing with it she was very happy with herself and how she viewed life. She conquered one of her biggest hurdles and learned

to stop worrying about what others would think of her and freed herself from a very painful past.

"I could use all the advice you can give me!" Stella said. "Lately I have been thinking about my teenage days and it has been giving me horrible nightmares."

Cathy questioned her, "Do you want to discuss your memories of your teenage years with me? Then I can get a better understanding of what you mean."

Stella quickly dismissed it by saying, "Oh no Cathy, it's silly stuff, teenage kid stuff, that's all. There were some things I regret and would love to change." No one had any idea of her past except for her husband. Stella was indeed thinking of her teenage days, especially of the time when she was violated. Sometimes her feelings about that episode would come out of nowhere and rise up and the only way she knew how to deal with it was by pushing it all back down.

Stella couldn't compare her story with Cathy's. What Cathy went through was far worse than her situation was. It was hard for her to hear and heartbreaking to think someone had to endure that kind of abuse.

Cathy had spoken to Stella about her past a few years ago. Stella remembered the story very well and it changed the way she viewed abuse. What had happened to Cathy was beyond cruel. She was an only child and encountered shocking and gruesome exploitation.

"My abuse started at an early age," she recalls Cathy telling her. "I had an uncle who would watch me a lot because my parents were busy working, building up their new restaurant business, wanting it to succeed, and they spent many hours there. We didn't have any other family in town so my uncle would be the one watching me.

"He lived on a farm not too far from us and when I would go over he would always have a new little toy for me. He was willing to do crafts with me and let me watch and do whatever I wanted—under one condition. I had to obey him and do what he asked me to do. There were a lot of sexual incidents. He would make me watch adult material on television with him and I would have to sit beside him as he watched and rubbed my leg.

"I hated to watch it. I was about nine years old and I remember thinking that it was so awkward watching it and watching it with him. I hated him for making me do that, hated him for what he put me through, and hated that my parents trusted him and put me into this situation in the first place.

"I felt trapped because he was a family member. I thought my parents should know who to trust to take care of me. I had so much shame and guilt that I couldn't stand myself when I was at his house. He was a heartless inhuman person. When I knew it was time to go to see him, anxiety and fear would take over my whole body as we drove to his house and I'd get very quiet. If I tried to speak my stutter would begin and I couldn't control it, I would be so agitated. My dad would be the one driving and he'd tell me, 'It's just for a bit. Mom will pick you up as soon as she can.' My dad didn't realize what was happening at his brother's house and that it was going to affect me for many years to come."

Stella asked her, "Did they ever find out about the abuse?"

"Yes. I talked to them many years later, I was an adult when I talked to them and they seemed to make light of it all. I got the sense they may have known some of what had happened to me but it was never made to be a big deal.

"That confused me tremendously. It made me think that I was the one blowing things out of proportion but I knew in my heart that was ridiculous. I found out that my uncle gave my parents the money they needed to start the restaurant. They felt like they couldn't turn their backs on him. He gave them a lot of money. Thankfully I had a great friend who had gone through abuse as well and was able to help bring me past the pain that I felt, also made me see, oddly, that the pain was a gift, which empowered me to grow into my higher self. This friend had many struggles and taught me a lot about how to look at things differently. There are always two sides to everything."

"Wow! Cathy, you are incredible!" Stella sighed. "You seem to talk from a place that is at peace with your past." She felt pain for her client, she had known her for many years and always knew of her abuse, but now she seemed to be ready to share her whole story with her. She explained to her if she shares her story with Stella and others, it would help her heal. The more she shared the more she would heal. She didn't feel sorry for Cathy, instead she felt proud of her and respected her for being so strong, and I think she could sense that.

"There are a few incidents that I remember that were the worst for me. My uncle had a gun and he would use it to hunt. He thought it was funny to try and hit birds as they flew in the air or targets that he would set up on the farm. One day he came up with an idea he said I might like. He asked if I wanted to try to shoot a target. I thought it would be kind of fun, so we set up a bucket of water and when we shot the bucket the water would flow out of it."

She took a deep breath and continued, "He ended up helping me hold the gun properly, holding me close and wrapping his arms around me to help me aim. I knew instantly this was getting him excited. I tried to tell him I was done with the gun and he told me that it was his turn with it. He then led me into the barn and told me to take off my clothes. I thought he was going to do his usual thing, touching me or making me touch him. I hated every second of it, and whenever I tried to move he would pull me back towards him.

"His plans that day were different, the barn threw me off, I thought it was odd. He told me to lie down and I felt something cold go inside of me, I remember being in utter shock. I realized he was using the gun. I was in a state of extreme shock and praying that it would be over soon. I remember thinking that if the gun went off I would die, and I didn't want to die. I should have wanted to die to get rid of all the pain but I didn't. If I died I wouldn't have to think anymore, but I also knew that one of these days I would be somebody, somebody who would inspire other people who have gone through abuse.

"The one thing my parents always told me was, 'You are such a special person. We knew when you were born that you would grow up and do great things with your life. We just know and believe that you will change many lives.' "

"He kept telling me he was doing this for me because my parents had asked him to take care of me, and this is why I might have forgotten about some of the events. He always gave me excuses as to why he had to do things to me. He said it was for my own good. I have no idea how long I was there or if anything else happened that day. I am okay if I never remember any more. The things I blocked out are meant to stay out of my mind, if I need to remember them they will come to me at some point."

Stella's heart ached for Cathy and she wanted to help her out in some way. She stopped cutting her hair and gave her a hug, those hugs always seemed to help. There was just something about a good hug from someone who accepts you fully and would love you no matter what you told them.

"Stella, thanks for that," Cathy said. "I've come a long way. I am good now! I have come to love who I am and know that I'm worth it and deserve all the goodness I have in my life. Even with these events that happened to me, I have finally found my own happiness."

Cathy's cell phone was ringing, she answered it and that left Stella in amazement from what her client went through and how she overcame it. Her mind was far away from what she was doing, she felt that familiar feeling of emptiness soar through her body.

"Sorry I had to take that call." She continued, "When I got older I stopped going over to his house. However, I started to feel as though something was missing and one day it hit me, I was missing the pain. I recognized I was used to feeling pain and turmoil. It might sound crazy to you, but I was used to that feeling and suddenly it was gone.

"I was searching for some sort of 'pain'. The people who were in my life weren't giving it to me. They treated me great, so I started to inflict pain upon myself. I thought that injuring myself would release the tension associated with strong emotions I had to deal with. At times I cut and burned my skin, as a temporary but intense feeling of punishment that was now missing from my life. It filled in that empty gap. I knew it was ridiculous, and it made no sense to me, but it felt good in the moment to treat myself like this. And as I got older I also started drinking a lot, I was sedating my emotions," she confessed.

"I understand what you are saying," Stella agreed. "I can see why you did that to yourself. You were punishing yourself, and you had shame and guilt you were dealing with. It's a vicious cycle that you got caught in. I get it, completely!"

Stella understood how Cathy was feeling. Many times she thought of doing things to herself to feel the pain that she thought she deserved. And she too got into drinking years ago as well. When something would trigger her she turned to polishing off a bottle of wine, it eventually became a nightly event. It was her need to reach for something outside of herself, to fill the void left inside of her. It was the quickest and most instantly pleasurable way for her to block out the horrible memories.

"Yes it was a vicious cycle for sure! My mom's words kept returning to me and it kept me from injuring myself even more," Cathy added. "The words that she repeated constantly to me were that I was going to be someone big, and that I was going to be somebody who made a difference one day. She told me I would be an inspiration. I began to heal myself by writing myself a letter about all the hateful thoughts I had of myself, I needed to get it out in paper and then I burned it, to allowed myself complete freedom to write whatever I wanted. No one else but me will ever see it, so I wrote down everything, all my core feelings that I felt about the people who had hurt me and the relationships with them.

"I wrote about why I felt the way I did. For me, this was a very powerful emotional healing technique. Do your best not to feel any shame or guilt about what you write—you are allowed to express your emotions in this way. Don't suppress or deny the way you feel, and get it all down on paper. No one will be judging you.

"The letter was symbolic. I cried and I remember being very scared to gain complete control of my life.

It should have excited me, but I wasn't used to being in control of my emotions and even my life. Amazingly, I reunited with an old friend of mine, our souls connected so perfectly, I could trust and tell this friend everything, and he made a very big positive difference in my life. There was no judging, I opened my heart and gave him a part of me and this friend accepted mine unconditionally." Cathy emphasized her words and I understood how grateful she was to have this kind of friendship.

This hit Stella hard. Her client had been through a horrible experience and yet had turned her life around. It astonished Stella. "Cathy, you have inspired me so much, you have taught me to see that whatever your situation you may be in, we can always pull out of it if we are willing to make the change within ourselves. Your self-confidence has completely changed and it shows, you are glowing and seem to be walking on air, you're so free!" Stella marveled.

Cathy was a true inspiration to Stella. The stories and experiences that we hear from others can teach us a lot about ourselves. When you are open-minded, you can learn better ways to deal with your own experiences.

It had been just over a year since the traumatic birth. Something had awakened in Stella on that day she couldn't make sense of. Her son's birth was a trigger that she would eventually realize was a blessing to set her free. Emotions and feelings kept creeping up through her body and she felt as though she was going to explode. This continued everyday, the intense rumbling of emotions had activated a volcano within her. There was a shaking inside of her that was like the molten rock (lava) within a volcano, and it was starting to billow out. Slowly, bit-by-bit, as she shared her past experiences with her friend Sara and began to describe to her how she was feeling and how she felt her whole life, the lava began its release.

Little did Stella know that by doing this, very soon an explosive eruption would take place, and in the end, eventually destroy the volcano. Although, once it gets destroyed there are still remnants of it on the ground, but the height and weight of it would be gone. Anything in the path of the emotional lava flow would be compelled to move out of its way, the determination and force of the inner volcano would not hold back or wait for anyone once it began to explode with its full force.

Sara listened to Stella over the course of several months and gave her advice based upon her experiences. She told her to follow what she needed to do in order to heal, and not worry about what others were thinking. It was her choice to heal and move forward and do this for herself, explaining to her that once she made the choice to move along on her journey it was important to keep going until she felt like she had come to a point where she was strong and in control.

"Focus on what you can do for yourself today, not on what you could've or should've done yesterday.

Think of it this way, for everything you've lost, you've gained something else. Life does not have to be perfect and wonderful when you are healing. Just count your blessings, not your troubles and soon enough you will make that switch."

Stella knew Sara was right. She had let many people control her life and she also let her reaction to situations control how she felt but now it was her time to stop burying and hiding her pain. She made herself a promise she wouldn't hold the past against herself.

Stella wrote in her journal, my past problems, my weaknesses, setbacks, and regrets are meant to teach me something. I chose to heal and because of this I will encourage others to do the same. I will make a dramatic change in my life and as a result of this I will be free and happy.

She felt an overwhelming desire to learn the meaning of her regrets and in doing this she approached everything as a lesson to be learned. She began to give attention to what she wanted to change about herself and wrote it all down. Suddenly, just by doing this something inside of her became activated and she stood taller, felt lighter, and had hope. Her heart started beating, she became emotional and a slight smile grew across her face.

In that moment she connected with herself and made a choice to follow through with this and heal. She knew there would be ups and downs but she was ready to face whatever came her way once and for all. She believed her clients saw her as she was meant to be—strong and confident not a scared little girl that she saw. Without even knowing it, Stella was already in the process of becoming the person she had always dreamt of being, but there was still a missing piece to this puzzle.

Stella regretted some of the decisions she had made in the past, but this decision felt so right. For the first time in her life she was going to face this once and for all. She wanted to stop being so hard on herself, make her own decisions, find out why she did the things she did and above all else she wanted to change the way she saw herself—she was going to develop in her mind the person she wanted to become.

She did so with the best knowledge and experience she had at that time, still she felt like something or someone was missing for her to fully gain an understanding how to properly do this. The decisions she made with her younger mind were made using the belief systems that others put on her at an early age, which changed how she viewed herself. Stella knew from now on, with her new wisdom and outlook she had of herself, she had the ability to choose differently and take control of her life.

Sara resumed, "Give yourself a break. Time and experience has a wonderful way of helping us grow and learn to make better choices for ourselves and for those we love and care for."

During the next nine months there were plenty of ups and downs. Harsh realities set in and she learned more about her past that she had forgotten and blocked out. The whispers in her head were pulling her back to the past several times, the outcome to all this was—she got thrown off balance a great deal. If she wanted to change, if she wanted to let go and move on with her life, she was the only person who could make it happen. It was her decision to make. She had to own her choices and take responsibility for her actions, own it and live though all the painful moments that would come along.

Stella told herself over-and-over, "I will accept the changes I know I need to make in order to heal." She found that life can be like a balancing act, as people are busy with work, kids, school, family, and so on, yet on top of this she found that there was also a perception obstacle that she needed to change. Continuing to always move forward while this is still happening will make you grow, this was the crucial key. Others had told her that in order to make the right choices we must help ourselves. Moving forward involves evaluating the clues we encounter, whether we chose to ignore them or not is completely up to us.

One day, as Stella recalled, she was having a particularly hard day with her journey. When the bad days came they consumed every thought and action she took. It was as if a negative presence was on the inside of her body and wouldn't leave until it was dealt with. A few months had passed on her healing journey and the way she could deal with it was through talking to Sara or her husband. Their support was invaluable and she trusted them completely, they loved her, no matter what.

Sara was talking to Stella on the phone one night and told her, "All relationships, jobs, and even people have an ending date. Sometimes we hold on to those people when it's not working out of fear that we won't be able to readjust to the necessary changes. The result is always the same, when we don't listen to what we want it leads to more pain, frustration, and regret." She pleaded to Stella, "Be smarter than that. Embrace the changes you know you need to make to move forward. Keep it simple and start with baby steps."

This resonated with Stella. She fully understood the need to have people in her life who helped lift her higher, on the other hand she knew it was very important to be able to learn to do it on her own as well, it must come from within. She needed to do this for herself, and by doing this it would benefit all areas of her life. Her husband and kids would see the real Stella, and she wouldn't have to feel as if she were hiding anymore. Jacob knew that once she healed she would be able to live happily and free. She was very grateful that her husband and their sons brought an immeasurable amount of joy into her life and just the thought that she could feel inner peace in herself excited her enough to keep moving on.

During the next couple of weeks she continued that push-pull. It was a struggle as she realized that this journey might be one that would take a long time. She wanted to move faster through it, but didn't know how. She was told that she needed to feel the pain and move through it at a steady pace, that was part of the process. Still Stella believed and had that nudging feeling that there was more that she could do to move through at an accelerated rate. She didn't want years of her life to go by and still feel that she was still dealing with these same issues.

MEET STELLA'S MENTOR ...
Jacob had a work function to attend and invited Stella along. He would often bring her out to these workshops so she would be able to understand how his business was structured in case Stella had to do the paper work for him.

The speaker at this particular function was Murray, a successful entrepreneur, coach and keynote speaker, his personal stories spoke out to Stella so much that day that it felt like she was the only one in the room. He went through all kinds of horrible situations and was able to turn his negative life around and this drew Stella to him and his ideas. Her instinct told her this was what she was searching for, the missing piece to her puzzle. After the event she asked Jacob to give Murray her contact information so they could talk to him further and learn more about the program he had to offer.

Shortly after that he sat in their home explaining to them how he became who he was and how he could help them out. He was sincere when he spoke it felt as though his words were speaking directly at Stella, she had a hard time understanding at the time that he was meant to be there. The past few months she had known that something was missing. She focused so strongly on her intuition that someone would be brought into her life and teach her how to create new habits and create a new self-image.

Murray became a dear friend, a mentor, and someone who she could trust. As their friendship grew she noticed that he led by example, had integrity, listened carefully, and had a desire to help others succeed. Murray had experience in what she was looking for and he was willing to share his skills, knowledge, and his expertise with her.

Murray is the one who was mentioned at the beginning of this book, when Stella stood in her kitchen, leaning against the counter, tears streaming down her face, sobbing hysterically, unable to catch her breath. Where she had received a phone call from this friend and her husband told her to answer it, because talking to him would help her.

This brings us to this point in her life, where Stella thought the explosive crying was what she needed to do to finish off her journey to heal. However, that was just the start of an incredible transformation that she had only dreamed about and now she was in its beginning stages. This man had the answer to Stella's prayers about wanting to accelerate her healing.

Stella absorbed what her friend had taught her very quickly—we get what we need the exact time we are supposed to receive it. We put out into the world, our ideas and perceptions of certain situations, what we ask, talk, and believe we receive, always.

Over the years Stella had no idea she could control or had power over her own inner thoughts. She didn't know that the people or circumstances around her didn't have to control her outcome. This whole time she held the key elements in her own head to remove the skulls from her tree. She realized that there is no other person who can control her thoughts, only she could do that, although, she hadn't been ready to face them until now. That's what true freedom is, being able to take control of your own thoughts.

Her friend urged her to listen to him carefully, "People come into our lives for all different reasons. We form relationships, but not all last. Some people come into our life temporarily, to teach us something. They come and go and make a difference."

She had learned this lesson over the years with her clients and friends. They have all given her great advice and shared stories that helped her see things differently.

He continued, "Sometimes we feel odd to have spent a lot of time with certain individuals and then suddenly find we are no longer connected to them, but that's exactly how it's supposed to be. We are always exactly where we are supposed to be, and also remember it is okay that they are not in our life anymore. The lessons the relationships with these people bring us make a difference in our life, if we learn to open our heart and mind.

"Even the people who enter our lives and drive us mad or break our trust can teach us something worthwhile. Then we'll meet new people again and the same thing will happen, either they'll stay in our life forever or they'll stay for a short period, just to teach us something."

Murray taught Stella many incredible lessons as she opened up to him over the course of the following few weeks. He taught her that just because she was struggling on certain days didn't mean she was failing. Every great success, big or small requires some type of worthy struggle if one is to achieve it.

He wanted Stella to express her feelings and not suppress them, he began to explain, "When you are struggling and come out of it, that's when you grow stronger and will gain more out of your need to learn we can all change for the better. It might be the most difficult thing you ever do, but it will be worth it. We are meant to live our lives to the fullest, and we're meant to be happy on the inside." Murray didn't judge her at all. He saw the potential and strength inside of her, which she would need to complete this course of her healing. His belief in her was enough to keep her moving forward.

He smiled and continued to tell her "Most of your fears are much bigger in your mind and as soon as you face them you'll see that this is true. The image that you have in your mind can be changed, you just have to recreate it in your head, have a clear picture of it and believe that you will succeed."

This excited Stella and she was ready to begin. The fear of facing her past and finding out who she really is, was a struggle for her. At first, it felt like a punishment but another important aspect of his advice was to listen to what her heart was telling her. She had to pay attention to her actual feelings and follow where they led her. "When you're following your inner voice and it makes you feel good, doors tend to open for you, even if you explored them before and they slammed shut on you, maybe before you didn't pay attention to how what your body was saying." he told her.

"You must give yourself permission to follow the path that makes you happy and with this you must realize that some people in your life will refuse to be beside you. As you start on your journey, they simply won't approve of what you are doing no matter what you say. Sometimes when you commit to creating your own happiness, it clashes with the perceptions of others.

As you grow and achieve your goals you gain something great, though at times you have to let go of something else. Others will stand by you no matter what and respect your decision. Understand that what has happened in your past happened to you and not because of you. Actually, what will happen as well is that you will create curiosity and spark their attention and they will want to know what you are doing just like you noticed change in some of your clients as they went through their transformation in dealing with their past. And then you will gain a whole new set of people who will come into your life, once you start to do the inner work on yourself and become who you are meant to be new friends arrive because you are operating on a different level of awareness."

Stella was listening closely to everything Murray told her and she put his advice into action immediately. After a few short weeks everything he told her started to sink in and she made sense of it all, the changes she saw began to amaze her. They say everything comes to you as you need it people come in and out of your path for a reason, certain people are put on earth to simply guide and lead others along life's way, and he was the one who fell from the sky to help her see that it was possible to live happily. She caught a glimpse what she was capable of, and when she understood that, his belief in her and also his encouragement, that was all she needed to begin.

He had spent some time talking to her and helping her through her pain, never rushing her. "Too many people overvalue what they are not and undervalue what they are," he spoke gently, "Don't be one of them. The past is now behind you. Focus on what you can do today to better yourself. Appreciate what you have and who you are today. The world needs you, I believe in you. You must dare to dream, in a world filled with disbelief, you must dare to believe, believe you are capable of doing anything you want. And once you do, I promise, you will find that power you once thought you lacked."

Everything he said to Stella made sense. It clicked, and through her pain she saw that just around a short bend she was about to heal and blossom into what she was meant to be.

"Promises are often left unfulfilled when making a promise to yourself. This could mean there is an uphill battle and a commitment, taking a chance in order to obtain what you want out of life. Wouldn't it be amazing to see your words come back to enhance your power? Wouldn't you love to know how to change your habits that are holding you back from moving forward?"

He was teaching her with his questions, Murray now knew her long enough to know her strengths and weaknesses, he wanted to see her succeed. Stella nodded, listening carefully to every word he was able to give her, his constructive feedback made her aware of what had been holding her back for so many years.

"You must be careful how you speak to yourself, words you hear can be twisted into any shape but you have the ability to accept or reject them. Your mind is powerful; we are all powerful creators of our own destiny. Remember this when you make a commitment to yourself as you start to change your self-image. The promises that you make to yourself must be backed up by devoted actions. The image you have of yourself in the future depends on the actions you take today, right now, in this moment. Commit yourself to do it, and then honor that promise! Commit to change the image you have of yourself, this is the key to the freedom you have been looking for."

Murray gave Stella the tools she needed and she began her life changing process. She started to study herself, looking at how and what she wanted to change in every aspect of her life. Every week that passed brought a new discovery and a higher state of accomplishment, as it became clearer and clearer who she wanted to grow into. She didn't like the word victim or survivor to describe her, the abuse that she had experienced had made her who she was. Stella liked the word BRAVE! Because it's so darn brave to forgive. Brave to live your life. Brave to hold your head high. Brave to recreate a new self-image of yourself.

Conclusion

TO THIS DAY, Stella still battles with mental hurdles that come with old beliefs and feelings about herself, but they come up far less and she can dismiss them rather easily now.

I am Stella! And growing up I only saw what I wanted to see and hear what I wanted to hear. But as an adult I am able to take matters into my own hands and change them. When I was younger I didn't understand I was able to control my thoughts, I made assumptions and believed that the abuse I experienced was what I deserved. Many times I viewed this body I live in as something that worked against me, including my mind.

Today it is simple for me to move my emotions from feeling vulnerable, shamed, or fearful to secure, calm, and deserving. An approach that I carry deep in my heart that has changed my perception is my willingness to improve myself at every opportunity. I created a new image of myself and began to move towards it. I aim to reach whatever goal I desire and have the belief in myself to do anything I want. I reach higher at every opportunity I have, I am done settling for average. I am now in charge of creating a life I have always imagined and inspiring others through my energy. I chase what I want now and I am not afraid, chasing what I am worth, not running away, no barrier will ever stop me.

What Murray taught me is that I could do the same as he did and you can do the same as well. If you want something, you have to go out and get it yourself. You must create what you want in your mind. You must be willing and able to do whatever it takes to hold your dream and fly with it. When you get inspired by someone else, you need to realize we are all made up same way as they are. The only difference is that a successful person is focused on improvements, and maybe they fought for what they wanted harder than you did. Anyone can do what he or she wants. You must have complete faith it will happen, any doubt that enters your mind will hold you back. I am no different than anyone reading this. Anyone can overcome their inner negative beliefs and become who they truly desire to be.

My nightmare of the disfigured tree in my dreams has changed. The nightmares are very sporadic and the tree now is fully green and beautiful, on the rare occasion I dream of it. The tree has now shed the dark evil voices that spoke to me as I hovered over the top of it. I wonder about other people's "trees", particularly the way that people willingly accept the noise of the trees in their lives. Their perpetual conversations about changing the shape of their tree or quieting the noises of the rustling leaves won't make any imprint on their roots until they take action. Some trees rustle their leaves loudly but never take action to change their shape, while other trees are more reserved when their leaves are rustled. Their leaves change shape and form and their branches grow upward, reaching to the sky.

Not a day goes by that I don't count my blessings that I have met certain people in my life who have led me to happiness. For many years I had been stuck in negative beliefs about myself, beliefs that have pulled me into the ground, and I'd never quite broken the surface to reach the sunlight, being caught in a world of darkness and isolation. Like some unfortunate seeds, I had grown not toward the sunlight but deeper into the dark earth. Also, like some seeds through desperate struggles I was finally able to break free into the sunlight. This does not ensure the seeds or my ultimate success, but now we at least we are motivated by our harrowing experience to make the best of our new opportunity for life.

One day there was a terrifying storm brewing in the sky. The little sapling, so small and delicate, discovered very quickly that it had to face and survive horrific weather conditions: tornadoes, rain storms, heavy snow falls, and even the deadliest, being struck by lightning. Although tiny, it had the strength to bend and not break, and endure whatever life had in store for it. The tree did, in fact, get through all types of challenges.

In times of stress, trees do not grow beyond their ability to support themselves. They start to shed leaves and branches in order to preserve their strength. So over the years, as this tree grew, it survived, but looked a little different from the rest. Its trunk was cracked and split, and parts of the woody branches looked injured, but still it has grown for many years.

The bark that protects the tree's trunk was mostly now removed due to humans carving and picking at it, leaving scars on it, scars that will forever remain on the trunk for all to see. But amongst all this, its roots underground extended three times the tree's width, making sure it was well-nourished.

The day had finally arrived where the tree has reached an age where it is able to flower. Humans have come out of nowhere to water, love, and hug the tree, something it needed so desperately in years past to encourage it to grow. The people's love for this tree has reminded it why it was first planted there and why it needed to stay. People need this tree to breathe. It was producing pure oxygen and helping to make a more beautiful landscape.

So many people go through life standing tall and being a tree with their roots in the ground and letting the wind just shift them back and forth, not doing anything else. I have broken through the surface of darkness that was piled on top of me and have readied myself to fight any storm that hits me. I am ready to feel the sun shining on me and let the wind rustle the leaves on my branches loud enough to inspire others. My hope and dream is for you to do the same.

Break through that barrier and create new ones for you and for others to learn from. Get back up and live life because every second, EVERY SECOND, not doing what you want is time wasted, time that you will never see again. You can become whatever you dream of, but it must come from within you. Go and fight for it.

Photo by Paula Bell Photography

About the Author

MONICA DA MAREN was born in Guelph, Ontario, to immigrant Italian parents. Having suffered abuse as a teen, she turned to writing as a form of therapy and self-awareness.

Through the joy of recording her thoughts and feelings she found healing and peace, and is now raising her own family with her loving husband of 12 years.

Monica has been greatly influenced by bestselling author and star of The Secret, Bob Proctor. To further her personal development she completed his intensive six-month coaching program with the guidance of Doug Dane, and is now proud to call him a friend and a mentor.

Today as a successful hairstylist and life coach,- Monica inspires her clients and others to release their painful past, follow their hearts and live their lives with authentic passion and purpose.

In addition to her writing, speaking and coaching, Monica has been a successful hair stylist for 18 years. After nearly two decades of making people's heads look beautiful on the outside—she has dedicated her life to making them even more beautiful on the inside.

Monica's article, The Roots of Keeping Us Grounded, was published on Gail Goodwin's Inspire Me Today® web site. In addition, it was picked up and published by Care2, the world's largest community for good, which boasts a subscriber list of 27 million people.

The article's popularity has inspired numerous local schools to reach out and invite Monica to speak to their student body. You can read the full text of her moving article at: http://ow.ly/H8i9W.

17410601R00095